THE BRICKS 'N BLOOMS
GUIDE TO
A Beautiful &
Easy-Care
Flower Garden

STACY LING

TEN PEAKS PRESS®
EUGENE, OR

This book is dedicated to my friends throughout the years who said they couldn't grow flowers. You can and you will. I got you.

XO

Cover design by Faceout Studio, Spencer Fuller
Interior design by Faceout Studio, Paul Nielsen

Photographs on pages 179, 212, and 224 by Maureen Nowak
All other photographs by Stacy Ling

For bulk or special sales, please call 1-800-547-8979. Email: Customerservice@hhpbooks.com

 TEN PEAKS PRESS is a federally registered trademark of the Hawkins Children's LLC. Harvest House Publishers, Inc., is the exclusive licensee of this trademark.

**The Bricks 'n Blooms Guide to a
Beautiful and Easy-Care Flower Garden**
Copyright © 2024 by Stacy Ling
Published by Ten Peaks Press, an imprint of Harvest House Publishers
Eugene, Oregon 97408

ISBN 978-0-7369-8848-3 (pbk.)
ISBN 978-0-7369-8849-0 (eBook)
Library of Congress Control Number: 2023936377

Printed in China

23 24 25 26 27 28 29 30 31 32 / RDS—FO / 10 9 8 7 6 5 4 3 2 1

Contents

Easy-Care Flowering Shrubs
page 125

Grow and Enjoy Hydrangeas
page 147

Container Gardening
page 169

Cut Flower Gardening
page 187

A Successful Easy-Care Garden
page 205

My Gardening Philosophy

While I'm an avid gardener now, I didn't grow up with a love for gardening. *Is that weird?* You'd think that for someone who's as into flowers and plants as I am, I would have been growing things my whole life, perhaps inspired by a talented gardener in my family, but that wasn't the case.

I grew up in a small suburban town—Livingston, in Essex County, New Jersey—where the properties were small and the houses were fairly close together. Our home was sited on a dead-end street and backed up to a babbling brook. Because the lot was pretty well-shaded and my parents both worked full-time, there wasn't a whole lot of gardening happening at our home. My brother developed some interest in gardening and planted a row of rose of Sharons along our driveway, but that was pretty much it.

During law school I met my husband, and our first home together was a small affordable housing condominium. We didn't own any property, just the condominium. At the time, my husband had just started his architecture career, and I had developed an interest in budget-friendly decorating and DIYs in the early days of my legal career in order to give myself a creative outlet. Since this was our first home and we had very little income, I was always looking for ways to make things pretty on a dime.

Our first home was sited between two townhomes and above another condo, and we struck up friendships with some pretty cool people in the neighborhood. One of my neighbors, Caroline, was *totally* into plants and flowers. And although her growing space was small, she planted *a lot* of unique, pretty blooms with different flowering times. She also had lots of beautiful houseplants. Her home was enchanting.

I started asking Caroline questions about all her plants and developed a genuine interest in growing some sort of garden, even though I lacked growing space and had no clue what I was doing.

My gardening journey began with a few houseplants in that tiny condominium. And I can honestly tell you that I did not achieve success with them. I repotted them, watered them, and tried to give them enough light, but they didn't survive. I wondered, *Was it me?* Maybe being a plant mom just wasn't my thing.

Now, I am not one to back down from a challenge, so I pulled myself up by my bootstraps and decided to try some outdoor gardening instead. I bought some pretty annuals to plant in a one-by-three-foot patch that led to our front door. It was a small, shady space that I could definitely handle. I consulted with Caroline about what to plant there. She recommended impatiens because they are easy to find, easy to plant, and easy to grow.

I shopped the local nursery and found some pretty light purple impatiens. After bringing them home, I planted them, watered them, fertilized them, and you know what?

They grew!

And so did my confidence as a gardener.

Because I had achieved that small success in a little one-by-three-foot patch of dirt, I decided to plant more annual flowers the following season around a small tree in the front yard that we shared with my downstairs neighbor. (She was okay with this, by the way.)

And you know what?

Those flowers bloomed too!

From that point on, I was smitten with gardening. And it wasn't too long after I achieved these small gardening successes that I begged my husband to move to a house with a little bit more land so I could grow a bigger garden.

After a few months of pleading, he agreed and we made the move to our suburban home in historic Chester, New Jersey, where we lived happily for the next twenty-three years.

From the moment we arrived at our new home, I planted every square inch of the foundation beds with annuals and quickly started working with perennials. I was eager and determined to grow flower gardens all over this half-acre property.

And wouldn't you know? Those gardens did really well. So, I started a new garden from scratch so I could grow more flowers.

As the years went on, I experimented with more plants, discovered new types of flowers, expanded my gardening spaces, created cozy outdoor gardening rooms, and even found some success growing indoor house-plants too.

So, what happened? How did I go from plant killer to plant parenting boss?

I discovered I had been working with the wrong plants.

They were the wrong plants for my home, my light conditions, and my life-style. Not all plants are created equal. Some are easy-care and some are just downright fussy. And if you are just starting out like I was? You will want to learn how to garden with an easy-to-grow, easy-to-care-for, low-maintenance approach.

Start small, achieve success, and grow your knowledge from there. Because knowledge doesn't just come from books, the internet, or a YouTube chan-nel. It comes from just doing. Learning the things that work. And learning the things that don't. What works for me may not work for you in your garden. But the only way to really know is by doing.

So, find your inspiration, do a little research, and just try things!

The key to becoming a successful gardener is not in knowing every Latin name and horticultural term for plants, but rather in finding joy digging in the dirt, nourishing your soul, and learning about the needs of various plants in your specific microclimate.

And don't take it to heart when a plant succumbs, because trust me, even the best gardeners lose plants every now and again. It's part of the process, and sometimes it just wasn't meant to be.

I subscribe to the "motel theory" of gardening: Some plants check in, enjoy their stay, and stick around. Others check in, don't love the location, and check out. When you take away the stigma of losing plants, it's much easier to grow your confidence as a gardener.

So, while you may or may not have killed plants before, by the end of this book, you will have the confidence to start, learn, and be successful at growing beautiful blooms.

You will walk away from this book with not only the ability to grow a beautiful flower garden, but you will also learn how to blend your garden with your home design to create a welcoming, cozy, and unique vibe.

Your green thumb starts . . . now!

CHAPTER ONE

Overview

———

Before we get started, I want to note that while this book focuses on growing flowers, you can apply a lot of the same concepts to growing vegetables and houseplants too. Don't feel limited by my focus on flower gardening. You can easily apply this same easy-care, low-maintenance approach to other types of gardening as well.

Chapter 2 focuses a little more on gardening basics and plant care. If you already know and understand the basics, feel free to use it as a reference and skip on to chapter 3, where we will chat more about garden design and choosing the right plants for your space and lifestyle.

And if you just need some quick tips and motivation? Head to chapter 11, because there you'll find inspiration that will fire you up.

About Growing Flowers

Growing flowers is a rewarding experience that nurtures and feeds the soul. With the hustle and bustle of our culture, together with life's daily stressors, the act of growing flowers can bring inner peace and give us a deep connection to the earth as we help make the world a more beautiful place.

When you think about it, flowers not only appeal to our sense of beauty but also carry deep symbolic meaning. We give flowers to loved ones to express our feelings, send them as a sign of celebration or bereavement, or decorate our homes with beautiful bouquets that breathe life into otherwise empty spaces.

Flowers create a certain mood or feeling, depending on the colors and textures chosen. Blues, purples, and pinks reflect peace and tranquility, while reds, oranges, and yellows kick things up and bring a sense of warmth and energy.

When choosing flowers for your garden, you'll want to consider the mood you want to create as well as considerations such as plant size, color, texture, bloom time, and fragrance (if any). The size and shape of the garden will also play a part in deciding which flowers and plants you choose to grow.

When I plan my gardens, I consider all of the above together with how *easy* the plants are to grow. Particularly when my kids were younger, I did not have the time to focus on staking top-heavy flowers and digging up tender plants for winter. Simply put, I needed a set-and-forget approach to flower gardening where plants would grow and bloom with ease with the least amount of work from me.

If this sounds like you, too, you are going to love this book. And with that, let's dig into how to plan your own beautiful, easy-care flower garden.

Know Your Gardening Zone

The first step to becoming a successful flower gardener is understanding your climate. I speak with a lot of newbie gardeners, and most of them don't know their hardiness zone. However, it's very important to know this before

---

Not sure what hardiness zone you are in?

You can check it here:

https://plterhardiness.ars.usda.gov

---

purchasing plants and growing a garden. Not all plants will thrive in all hardiness zones, and certain perennial plants—which tend to be more expensive—may not return because they are not hardy to that zone.

You probably realize that the climate in Florida is much different from, say, the climate in Wisconsin. But the hardiness zone map goes deeper than that. Even northern New Jersey has a different hardiness zone than southern New Jersey. So, it's important to know what your zone is.

Learn Your First and Last Frost Date

Your hardiness zone will guide you to the first and last frost date for your microclimate. A frost date is the average date of the first and last light freeze in spring and fall for a particular zone. And that first and last frost date is significant because it tells you what to plant and when.

For example, I grow flowers, herbs, and vegetables in gardening zone 6a. Some flowers, like dahlias, are not hardy here. They are considered tender, which means frost and cold weather will kill them off. So, if I want to grow them the following season, I need to dig up the tubers, store them inside in a cool, dark place, and replant them the following year. Or I need to treat them like annuals and purchase new tubers for the next season.

Not all garden flowers work this way, but dahlias are a good example as to why those frost dates matter. As an aside, if you are just starting to garden with flowers, I don't recommend growing dahlias at first, because they are a little more work.

Typically, your local nursery will carry plants and flowers that can be grown in your specific microclimate. Just understand the differences between what is annual and what is perennial in your hardiness zone (see chapters 4 and 5). If you are unsure, ask the nursery staff, check with an experienced gardening friend, or reach out to your local cooperative extension.

And if you order seeds or starts from a plant catalog, read the description well so you know what can be grown successfully in your zone.

Garden Tools and Supplies for the Beginner

Before we start gardening, we need to stock up on a few basic supplies that every gardener uses. From pruners to hand trowels, garden forks to shovels, what do you need to live your best gardening life?

It can be overwhelming and costly to try to buy everything you will need all at once. However, there are some basic tools and supplies every gardener uses that you should invest in.

BEGINNER TOOLS

Hand trowel	Garden fork	Garden rake
Pruners	Spade shovel	Wheelbarrow
Garden gloves	Garden shovel	

My list of supplies could go on and on, but these are the basic things you need to get started.

Note: If you lack growing space and are gardening with containers only, you may not need to purchase the larger tools and supplies, like the garden fork, spade shovel, garden shovel, garden rake, and wheelbarrow.

Find the Right Location

Before you start planting, spend some time observing your light conditions. I know how hard it can be to go to the nursery, because you want to just take home every pretty flower there to have in your garden. But trust me, your success will depend on understanding your landscape's light conditions.

Not all plants are suited for full sun. And not all plants are suited for shade. If you purchase plants that require full shade and you plant them in full sun, they'll scorch, look terrible, and likely die—and then you'll walk away feeling like a failure.

So, instead of wasting money on plants and killing your confidence, understand the light conditions you have *before* you buy. When you are at the nursery, read the plant tags to see the type of light conditions each plant requires.

How can you tell what kind of light a certain spot in your landscape gets? Watch the area for one full sunny day, checking it hourly from morning through evening. And take good notes because trust me, you won't remember!

If your garden space gets 6 to 8 hours of sun, that is considered "full sun." If the space gets 4 to 6 hours of sun, that is called "partial sun" or "partial shade." Anything below 4 hours of sun is considered "shade." Keep your conditions in mind when you read those plant tags, *before* you purchase anything. Nursery growers are telling you exactly what that plant needs to grow, bloom, and thrive. Having that knowledge will help you plant a garden that is best suited for your growing conditions.

And this applies to any type of gardening you do. Whether it's flowers, vegetables, or houseplants, it's important to understand the light conditions you have.

Thus, if your outdoor garden space is heavily shaded, roses will not do well there, because they need full sun. You could want to grow roses all day long, but if they aren't getting enough sun, you won't find success.

So, do that little bit of work before you shop. Research the light requirements of your plants, and you'll save yourself a lot of heartache and money.

Figuring Out the Best Growing Conditions

Like I said before, even the best gardeners make mistakes, and everyone learns by doing. I mean, there are so many plants out there, and unless you have experience working with them, it's hard to really know and understand what they need.

As an example, I enjoy growing cilantro. But I was not always successful with it, and it took me the better part of twenty years to figure out why.

Nurseries stock up on and start selling cilantro plants in the spring, and I always used to buy them along with other herbs like parsley, basil, and rosemary.

Because cilantro plants are considered annuals here in New Jersey, I would wait to plant them until the last frost date, which is typically around Mother's Day. And year after year, I'd only get a month or so out of them. By the time July arrived, they'd all bolt and die.

Every. Single. Year.

It was so discouraging, and it got to the point where I thought it was me. Cilantro didn't like me, didn't like my garden, I couldn't grow it, so I wasn't going to try.

But then I thought it through and realized it behaved similarly to lettuce, which is a cool season vegetable that enjoys cooler temperatures in both spring and fall. Lettuce is not a fan of the heat, either, because it bolts in the summer and dies.

The lightbulb went on and I realized that cilantro is a plant that requires cooler temperatures. And now that I know that? I grow it successfully in the spring *and* in the fall.

To give you another example, for years I tried growing Boston ferns inside my home. They'd do well for a few months, but they would decline and then die. For the life of me, I could not figure out what I was doing wrong. I potted the plants in good soil, maintained them in optimal lighting conditions, and was careful not to overwater or underwater them, but they kept dying anyway in late winter or early spring.

Eventually, I stopped trying to grow Boston ferns and simply believed that they just did not like me. In fact, I used to tell people that ferns and I were 100 percent *not* friends and never would be.

After several years, though, I thought a little more about it and realized that maybe my home did not provide them with the right growing climate. Boston ferns love humidity, and my home was very dry during the winter. And looking back, I recalled that they'd succumb near the end of every single winter.

Once I realized that, I tried my hand at growing Boston ferns again. Because I had to prove to myself that I could do this, I purchased another Boston fern and also bought a humidifier to add some humidity to the indoor air during the winter.

And you know what?

That fern survived. It didn't look amazing, but it survived. And once I got it back outside in the summer humidity, it thrived and is still looking great today.

Don't get down on yourself if you don't always find initial success. I know it's hard not to sometimes, but spend some time troubleshooting why the plant didn't do well. Ask yourself, *What does this plant need to thrive?* Think through what you are offering in terms of climate and light conditions. And if you notice something that's less than ideal, try to find a way to fix it. Chances are, some need is not being met. And that is how we learn to become better gardeners.

Sometimes we can't give a plant what it needs because it's just not suited for our home and garden. And that is okay. Learn to be okay with that and move on to plants that are better suited for your space.

Three Easy Ways to Start a Flower Garden

Whether you have a large gardening space or not, there are a few different ways you can start a flower garden from scratch.

The Traditional Method

If you are planning to create a new in-ground garden bed, the best way to start is to grab a shovel, pitchfork, and wheelbarrow, and start digging out the grass.

- Choose a location based on what you want to grow and the light conditions you'll need.

- Lay out the new bed by marking its dimensions with a hose or long extension cord.

- Use a spade shovel to follow the outline of your planned garden bed and slice through the grass roots while making sure you dig out all the grass and roots. You can replant the grass elsewhere or add it to a compost pile. But you can also find a small spot on your property, flip it over, and allow it to decompose.

- Stand back and look at the outline you've just created. Does it look right? Adjust if needed, or if you love your new garden's size and shape, dig out the rest of the grass using the spade shovel, pitchfork, or both. Get all the roots so the grass does not grow back.

- Once you have fully dug out the grass, loosen and aerate the soil by pitching or turning it over so it's ready for planting.

The No-Dig Method

But what if you don't want to do the backbreaking work of digging?

There is an easier way to go.

If you've got some time on your hands and can wait a few months to plant, try using the no-dig method. It's easier on the back, plus it saves time and energy.

Similar to the digging method, mark out the dimensions of your garden. But instead of digging it out, flatten and lay cardboard boxes on your future garden plot. Add a few inches of mulch on top of the cardboard, then let time work its magic. Over the course of the next few months, the cardboard will break down beneath the mulch while the weight of it all kills and suppresses grass and weeds. You could use three to four layers of newspaper instead of cardboard, too, but I prefer cardboard because it is heavier and doesn't blow around.

You will want to clean up the border either before or after you complete this process, but I've used this method several times and it works like a charm! I've started mixed borders like this, too, by planting flowering shrubs in the ground first, laying cardboard around them, mulching on top, and then voila! I have a whole new garden!

While you can use weed block landscape fabric instead of cardboard, I strongly suggest avoiding it. The weed block does not break down, which makes it more difficult to plant in the area later and it prevents flowers from growing as freely as they would without the barrier in place. Unless you make the effort to remove the fabric, it is not worth using in a flower garden.

Raised Garden Beds and Container Gardens

If you have less gardening space to work with or you want to start small, raised garden beds or small planters may be the way to go. We'll chat more about these in chapter 9.

There is something very satisfying about taking a plain patch of grass and turning it into something beautiful. I realize it sounds like a lot of work, but your patience and hard work will be rewarded every time you see those gorgeous flowers in your garden.

CHAPTER TWO

Gardening Basics

———

Before we dive into the fun stuff, it's important to understand some gardening basics because these principles and tasks can make or break a garden. That said, if you are familiar with the basics and don't need a refresher, feel free to move on to the next chapter and use this one as an extra resource or troubleshooting tool.

Now, let's start with essentials. Much like people need air, food, and water to live, plants are the same. To grow a garden that thrives, a plant needs:

- Sunlight
- Air
- Nutrition
- Water

It sounds pretty obvious, but in order to learn how to grow plants with success, we've got to keep this in mind. If one or more of those needs are not met, your plants will decline and eventually die.

It Starts with Good Soil

I can't stress this enough. Plants are fed by soil that is rich in organic matter and other nutrients. If soil quality is poor, plants, flowers, and other vegetation will struggle to flourish. Provide good-quality soil and you'll be rewarded with an abundance of blooms.

The Importance of Getting a Soil Test

If you've never done a soil test or aren't sure how good your soil is, there are test kits available through your local cooperative extension. Soil test kits can also be found at nurseries and through online retailers. These tests will tell you what's lacking in your soil so you'll know how you can correct it. If you don't understand the results, call your local cooperative extension, where a master gardener will be happy to explain it to you.

Why does soil composition matter? Well, some plants need certain nutrients and others may not. For example, shrubs like azaleas and rhododendrons prefer soil with higher acidity. If the garden location you plant them in has soil with low acidity, those plants won't thrive.

But all is not lost if you want to grow azaleas or rhododendrons and your soil is low in acidity. We can amend the soil to improve those conditions or choose to grow them in raised garden beds where we have more control over the quality of our soil. Or, instead of growing azaleas and rhododendrons, we might grow hydrangeas, since the acidity may only affect the color of the flowers instead of the plant's overall health.

Don't get too bogged down with the details, just know that having your soil tested provides you with information that can help you fix problems specific to your garden. *What kind of soil do I have?* is the first question to ask when troubleshooting why a plant fails.

Does every gardener do this? They should. If you opt to skip this step, you'll learn by doing. If that's your choice, that is okay. Just understand that what you plant may or may not do well. If the plant doesn't thrive, you'll feel like a failure, probably won't plant it again, or you'll wind up getting the soil tested anyway to help you learn what the soil needs so you can try again.

That said, if you are just starting out, purchase fresh garden or potting soil that is rich in organic matter, whether you're putting your plants directly into the ground or potting them in containers. The nursery staff can help you find the best options available.

About Soil Amendments

As you learn how to garden, it's a great idea to add compost, leaf mold, and other soil amendments that will feed your plants and improve the overall soil quality, structure, and drainage. Improving your soil seasonally, or even yearly, will help you grow a prettier and healthier garden. The first thing you'll start with is compost.

Compost

Compost is made when organic material like food scraps decompose over time. You want to add compost to your soil because it is high in nutrients that enrich overall soil quality, which promotes healthy plant growth.

Adding compost to beds and containers is a good way to feed your plants on a regular basis. Whether you top your garden off with compost in the spring and the fall or make a compost tea to add to your plants throughout the growing season, it's a more organic way to provide your plants with nutrition instead of using synthetic fertilizers. You can purchase compost at the nursery or make it yourself for free.

Compost Benefits

- Compost helps build good soil structure.
- It feeds earthworms and other microbes in the soil.
- Compost helps maintain a neutral soil pH level.
- It helps the soil retain moisture and air.
- Compost adds nutrients that keep plants healthy and protected from pests and disease.

If you are learning how to garden, I recommend buying compost from the nursery to add to your beds until you feel confident and ready to make your own. You can also look for garden or potting soil bags with compost already mixed in.

While it's super easy and affordable to make your own compost, it can be overwhelming to do it all if you are just learning the basics. As you achieve success in other areas of gardening, maybe you'll eventually want to take on making your own compost. For now, just understand how compost benefits your garden and plan to include it in your gardening ritual.

Leaf Mold Compost

Composted leaves are also a great soil amendment to add to garden beds and containers because they help improve soil quality and drainage. Composted leaves work as a soil conditioner that increases water retention and improves overall soil structure, helping plant roots stay cool and hydrated during hot, dry weather.

Composting leaves is simple to do, but the leaves take time to break down. When you rake your leaves in the fall, pile them in an area, dampen them thoroughly, mix them up, and let them decompose over time. But don't worry if you lack time or garden space to compost your own leaves. You can also purchase leaf mold compost at the nursery.

Composted Manure

Composted animal manure is another valuable soil amendment rich in organic matter that can supply nutrients for plant growth in your home garden. Make sure you only use composted manure from plant-eating animals such as cows, sheep, chickens, deer, and rabbits. Do not add dog, cat, or pig manure in gardens or compost piles, as those types of manure are too hot and will burn your plants.

To keep things simple, purchase bags of aged manure or find soil bags that already have the amendment mixed in.

Planting Basics

Planting your garden may seem a bit intimidating, but it doesn't have to be. Just by following a few simple steps, you can be on your way to your very own beautiful, easy-care garden.

How to Plant a Garden

1. Lay out your plants in the garden space. (See chapter 3 for design tips.) The new bed may look sparse the first year or two, but it will fill in over time, so space the plants accordingly. (It will be less work for you later!)

2. Using a shovel or hand trowel, dig a hole two times the size of the root ball for each plant.

3. Remove the plant from the plastic nursery pot, fanning the roots out with your fingers to encourage them to grow outside the root ball. If plants are rootbound, use a shovel or sharp knife to slice through the roots first, then fan them out with your fingers to loosen the roots. Don't worry about damaging the plant during this process because it helps the roots grow out into the soil and improves plant health.

4. Add fresh garden soil with amendments to the hole before planting.

5. Set the new plant in the hole, making sure the plant's soil surface lines up with the ground's soil surface.

6. Backfill the hole with fresh garden soil, amendments, and existing soil.

7. Top the bed off with fresh mulch.

8. Water well.

How to Read a Plant Identification Tag

A plant identification tag is a small label that provides important information about a plant. Understanding how to read a plant tag can help you make informed decisions when selecting plants for your home and garden. Information you'll find on a plant tag may include:

- The common name of the plant, like rose, hydrangea, or tulip

- The plant's scientific or botanical name, which may include the genus, species, and cultivar, like *Tulipa* 'Palmyra'

- Hardiness zone, which tells you if a plant is suitable for your climate

- Mature height and spread which indicates how tall and wide a plant will be at maturity

- Information on the growth habit of the plant, such as upright, spreading, or trailing, which can be helpful in determining where to plant it in your garden

- Information on the amount of light the plant requires, such as full sun, partial sun, or shade

- Watering requirements, including how often it needs to be watered and how much water it needs

- The type of soil the plant prefers, such as well-drained or acidic

- The time of year when the plant will produce flowers, if applicable

- Information about the foliage

- Information on any special features or attributes of the plant, such as fragrance, colorful berries, or attractive bark

By carefully reading the tag and considering the information it provides, you can ensure that you choose the right plants for your home and garden.

How to Maintain a Garden

Now that we've covered the importance of soil quality and planting basics, there are a few tasks a gardener needs to know how to do in order to cultivate and care for a beautiful flower garden.

Watering

Much like people, plants need water to survive. How much or how little a plant requires depends on the time of year it is and the type of plant you grow.

When growing plants outside, consider the natural growing conditions for that particular plant. For example, lavender prefers drier soil and climates, so planting it in a garden that has poor drainage and gets a lot of rain can be a recipe for disaster.

Know the different watering needs of your plants before you start to grow them, and group plants together based on their needs. This requires reading the plant tag (you'll hear a lot about plant tags throughout this book). While you can learn a lot about gardening through trial and error, just thinking things through before purchasing and planting can save a lot of money, time, and effort in the long run—not to mention, you'll keep up your confidence as a gardener!

How to Water

Regardless of the type of garden you grow, make an effort to water the bases of plants during the earlier part of the day. Watering in midday heat is not as effective because the water may evaporate before it is absorbed. But if you water in the cooler evening temperatures or at night, it can promote pest and disease problems because plants also don't absorb water as easily without sunlight. Also, watering at the base of the plant is best because water from above may not reach plant roots when the foliage is dense.

Admittedly, I have watered in the late afternoon on a rare occasion if I did not get a chance to water during the earlier part of the day. But that is not the norm. Make it a habit to water the base of your plants in the early part of the day, regardless of the type of garden you grow. Your plants will reward you with prolific blooms and good overall health.

Also, water plants deeply instead of giving them quick, shallow spurts of water because it encourages a deeper root system. How often you'll need to water depends on what plants you are growing, where you are growing them (sun or shade), and how you are growing them (in containers or in the ground). I also water my gardens differently, depending on the season. For example, a hot, dry summer will need more of my hands-on watering efforts than a cool, wet spring.

That said, a well-established perennial garden with shrubs and trees should be able to thrive on its own, for the most part. But where summers are extremely hot or dry, you'll need to supplement with deep watering if you don't have an irrigation system in place.

Annuals and container gardens will need care more or less often, depending on the weather—particularly during the summer. In the summer heat, these plants can easily get too dry, they'll bloom less, and their leaves can burn. So, make sure to keep a close eye on them. (See more about this in chapters 4 and 9.)

Fertilizing

When it comes to fertilizing, not all plants should be treated equally. And using more fertilizer is not always better. When using fertilizer on your plants, always follow the directions on the package.

For the most part, I rely on good organic soil amendments to feed my gardens. Since perennials, shrubs, and trees live for many years, feeding them with artificial nutrients acts more like a steroid than like actual nourishment. Therefore, perennials, shrubs, and trees generally don't need to be fertilized.

Synthetic fertilizers encourage these types of plants to produce quick, new shoots before they are naturally ready. Those new shoots are then more susceptible to pest and disease problems. So, unless they are grown in containers where the nutrients wash out every time you water, focus on having healthy soil more than on adding fertilizer.

However, there are instances where I recommend using a fertilizer in order to nourish my plants and encourage them to produce more flowers. Roses, annuals, container gardens, and houseplants can all benefit from being fertilized. You could just use compost to feed these plants, but some flowers require a little more nutrition to produce an abundance of blooms.

To keep the process simple, use a slow-release fertilizer, like Osmocote Smart Release or Proven Winners Continuous Release Plant Food. These products last several weeks to a few months, while a liquid fertilizer lasts a week or only a few days. It's a set-and-forget approach that means less work with the same results. Where roses are concerned, I prefer to use Espoma Rose Tone.

Just be sure to make a note on a calendar or set a reminder in your phone so you remember the right time to feed your plants again based on the package directions.

Mulching

Mulching garden beds helps suppress weeds and retain moisture, and the mulch will eventually break down to enrich the soil.

I add wood chips to my flower beds yearly, but I don't use any mulch in my container gardens because it's not necessary, especially if you pack them full with plants like I do.

If you choose to mulch plants or flowers that you want to eat (like vegetables, fruits, herbs or something like nasturtium blossoms), use cedar mulch or wood chips that don't contain arsenic. Arsenic, which should never be ingested, is present in many woods, and it can leach into the soil and be taken up into the plant by its roots.

Avoid mounding mulch around the trunks of trees and bases of plants, as this can promote pest and disease problems. Keep some space between the mulch and the tree trunks or plant stems.

Weeding

I know it's not a favorite garden chore, but weeding makes your garden beds look tidy while also preventing new weeds from starting. Plus, it helps plants stay healthy and look amazing in your garden. When beds are tidy, the entire yard looks more welcoming and attractive. And the more often you pull weeds, the easier the job is. So, keep up with it.

The best method for managing weeds is to use a combination of pulling individual weeds out by the root, applying a good layer of mulch to the entire bed, and planting smarter. To plant smarter, grow plants slightly closer together than you normally would to help crowd out weeds, or use ground covers in between plants to help keep weeds from popping up.

Walk through your garden every day, pull out weeds whenever you see them, and be sure to get at them from the root. I can't tell you how many mornings I'm outside walking around in my pajamas and slippers, coffee in hand, enjoying my flowers and pulling a few weeds. Believe it or not, it's actually less work for me this way and more enjoyable as I can take the time to admire my garden.

Don't wait too long to remove weeds, because they can get out of control pretty quickly. This is another reason why it's best to start with a small garden—it's more manageable to keep up with the weeding in a smaller space.

Avoid using weed block in flower gardens because weed block makes it more difficult for flowers to self-sow, and it doesn't really help with long-term weed suppression anyway. If you want to smother the weeds that pop up between flowering plants, I suggest using a few layers of newspaper with mulch, as this combination will kill the weeds now and will eventually break down to enrich the soil.

Staking

Flowers that get super top-heavy or grow really tall need additional support from rain, wind, and other inclement weather. To keep those plants from falling over, they may need to be staked. If you are new to gardening, you'll most likely start with grow-through hoops or single garden stakes.

Not all plants need assistance, but some definitely do. Consider the amount of work you want to do before planting varieties like dahlias, delphiniums, and hollyhocks that may need staking. Can you plant them without staking? Sure. But they may not look so good after a heavy rain.

Ways to stake plants:

- Using grow-through hoops
- Using single garden stakes
- Corralling
- Netting
- Trellising

So, if you are just starting out or want to grow a flower garden that's easy-care and low-maintenance, plant flowers that don't need extra support. We'll talk about what those flowers are in later chapters.

Keeping Plants Happy and Healthy

Dividing Plants

Dividing plants helps them stay healthy, keeps the garden looking good, and lets you share the bounty with others. It's not something you need to do every year, but it should be done every few years. We'll touch more on this in chapter 5.

Deadheading

Deadheading flowers means removing old growth and seed heads to encourage fresh growth and more blooms. When plants focus on seed production, they don't put out as many flowers. So, it's important to remove those seed heads in order to encourage more flowers to bloom.

Certain plants benefit from deadheading while others don't. And whether or not to deadhead largely depends on the flowers you grow. For example, salvia and catmint plants can get a second set of blooms if you deadhead spent flowers. But others, like columbines, hollyhocks, foxgloves, and forget-me-nots, self-sow and benefit from being left alone to do their own thing. Therefore, it's important to evaluate whether a plant requires deadheading or not before removing spent blooms.

When you see flower heads turning brown and not looking so pretty, it's time to start deadheading. I know this sounds like tedious work, but it's surprisingly therapeutic and relaxing to do. I have come to enjoy these small moments with my flowers.

How to Deadhead Flowers

As the blooms fade, use sharp pruners, snips, or your fingers to remove the flower stems just below the spent flowers and just above the first set of full, healthy leaves. Check your plants carefully to ensure that no flower buds are hiding among the faded blooms before you cut them off. You don't want to accidentally snip off future flowers!

CHAPTER THREE

Garden Design Ideas

———

Now that you have the gardening basics down, let's dive into the fun stuff: creating and designing a welcoming home with flowers that are easy-care and low-maintenance.

Flower gardening is an art. We start with a blank canvas, choose pretty plants that bloom throughout the seasons, and from there we can create an overall aesthetic for our homes.

There are a few ways I like to approach flower garden design to keep things simple yet beautiful. For example, choosing flowers that are low-maintenance and relatively pest- and disease-resistant will make things easier for you on a daily basis.

And you don't have to go all-in on a big garden to enjoy gorgeous flowers. You can easily apply these same design ideas to smaller beds or container gardens. Just scale back the overall concept.

Whatever you choose, consider how large an area you realistically want to maintain. Because if you don't maintain what you plant, the garden will get unruly, look messy, or, worse, die. Which is why I recommend starting small with easy plants if you are just beginning, want to dabble, or need to grow your confidence as a gardener.

Think through your lifestyle before you design, plant, and decorate your garden spaces to make it easier for you long term. Every spring it's tempting to want to do it all, but be realistic with how much time you have available to maintain your garden. You can always add more next year.

Creating a Welcoming Home with Flowers

Whether you go all-in on flower gardening or not, nothing says "welcome to my home" more than plants and flowers. Without them, a home lacks personality and life.

Foundation plants accessorize the front exterior of a home, making it inviting, warm, and cozy by softening the hard lines and adding some character. Even a few seasonal flowers planted in beds or in containers flanking the front door can create the perfect, cozy entrance.

As your gardening confidence and skills increase, consider adding more plants to outdoor living spaces like porches, patios, decks, and firepits. Potting a few seasonal annuals or bringing houseplants outdoors in the summer can make a huge impact by breathing more life into these spaces. Just keep in mind the light conditions needed for those plants before incorporating them into your outdoor landscape.

Flower Garden Design Ideas

While there are a number of ways to design a flower garden, I lean more toward informal cottage gardens that attract pollinators. To me, informal gardens that don't need to be meticulously maintained are a better fit for a busy life. And if they draw a few butterflies and hummingbirds in too, I'm all about it.

Since the best time to plant a garden is in the fall or spring, plan and prepare ahead before you plant. That said, we don't always know what will work in our gardens until we try it. So, in order to learn, try new things, stretch your knowledge, and just do. Adapt your garden's design to the growing conditions you have and the time you have available to spend working in the garden.

And keep in mind that the prettiest flower gardens don't happen overnight. They take time, so be patient with both your garden and yourself as you learn.

Where to Find Inspiration

Find local gardeners and see what they grow that's blooming throughout the seasons. Look at magazines, books, gardening websites, and social media. Visit your local nursery once a month (if possible) to see what's in bloom when.

All these methods are great sources of inspiration to find plants that could grow well in your garden. They also give you a sense of which colors, plant combinations, textures, sizes, and styles best speak to you.

Choose Native Plants

For the easiest garden to grow, choose native plants whenever possible. Native plants are accustomed to your local climate, as they've likely been growing there for hundreds, maybe even thousands, of years. They are more resistant to pests and diseases than non-native plants, they adapt easier, and they can generally take care of themselves with minimal help from you.

The range of native plants available depends on your locality. While some plants are tagged as native at nurseries, many aren't, so do a little research ahead of time if you want to grow plants that will thrive in your climate with little care.

General Garden Design Basics

- Consider your garden location so you can group plants with the same light and watering requirements.

- Conceptualize your garden design by making a mood board or creating a folder of flowers and designs you love.

- Think about bloom time, colors, textures, flowers, and foliage shapes.

- Create mixed borders with bulbs, annuals, perennials, shrubs, and evergreens.

- Plant according to spacing and height, with shorter plants in front and taller plants in back.

- Include a focal point like a fountain, obelisk, or bird house.

- Consider critter issues before planting. Deer, rabbits, groundhogs, and other wildlife all like to munch on plants. Determine if you will need to add fencing, or figure out another way to deter critters from your garden.

- Plant in odd numbers for an aesthetically pleasing design.

- Repeat the same plants and colors throughout your design so the garden flows and your eye is drawn fluidly throughout the bed.

Getting Started

Before designing and purchasing plants for any garden, measure your gardening space so you know what size plants it can accommodate and how many will be needed.

Also, consider the critters that abound in your area, because they can do a lot of damage in a short amount of time. There may be plants that look similar to the ones you want to use that won't succumb to wildlife as easily as others.

For example, where I live, deer are a huge problem. When I hone my plant list, I consider what plants the deer are less likely to eat. That's not to say I don't ever plant flowers that are less deer-resistant, because I do. But I need to keep up with spraying these plants with deer repellent, which is a little more work for me. I'm willing to do this, but it's much less maintenance to focus on plants the deer tend to leave alone.

Calculating Your Garden Space

If you are predesigning your garden space, you should calculate the garden area so you know how many plants to buy. Of course, you can always wing it at

the nursery. But if you want to understand the mathematics of garden design and be more precise (and probably save time and money), here's how to calculate how many plants will fit in your garden.

1. Measure the area with a tape measure to determine the length and width of your garden.

2. Calculate the area by multiplying the length by the width to get the total square footage.

3. Use plant tags to determine the recommended spacing between plants based on the size they will be at maturity.

4. Divide the total square footage of the garden by the recommended spacing between plants to determine the maximum number of plants that can fit in the area.

5. Depending on the shape of your garden and your desired garden design, you may need to round up or down to account for any gaps or spaces between plants. I lean toward rounding up, because there's always room somewhere for one more plant if I buy too many. I'd rather have extra plants than not enough.

How to Design an Everblooming, Colorful Garden

My approach to flower gardening is to create an easy-care design that will grow and change throughout the seasons. While it requires some thought, it's not difficult to achieve once you get to know your plants. The idea is to plant flowers with different bloom times, textures, colors, and foliage types so that something is always happening in the garden.

Choose different plants so that some start to bloom in early spring, others in mid-spring, late spring, early summer—you get the idea. The bloom times should overlap, if possible, so there's always something flowering in the landscape until winter arrives. And the longer the bloom time, the more you'll get out of that particular plant. So, if you gravitate toward easy-care flowers like peonies or irises that are short-lived, plant reblooming varieties or several different types of the same plant to extend their bloom time.

Beyond the time plants will bloom, look for plants and flowers that will provide color, texture, and interest throughout the growing season. This means looking at the blooms *and* their foliage, because plants with colorful foliage, like heucheras, continue to provide color in your garden even when the blooms are lacking.

Depending on the size of your garden space, consider planting a mix of evergreen shrubs and trees, deciduous flowering shrubs, perennials, bulbs, and annuals. This may be something you do before you start a new garden, or you can add these elements to an existing bed.

In your garden planning, think through how the garden will look throughout the seasons. Planting a mixed border with small evergreens provides year-round interest. Tuck in spring and fall annuals for instant seasonal color. Add spring-flowering bulbs for early spring color. As you gain experience, you'll learn when the gaps of blooms happen in your garden, and you'll find plants to fill that need.

The beauty of it is, you don't have to do it all at once. You can totally start small and do more and more as you learn and grow your confidence.

How to Get Year-Round Color in the Garden

Although certain climates experience cold, dark winters, that doesn't mean you can't continue the color in the garden year-round. While you may not be able to see blooms all year long, planting conical evergreen trees and small shrubs provides interest throughout the seasons, adds structure, and gives the eye a place to rest in the gardens.

But choose your elements wisely, particularly if you're planting next to or in close proximity to your home or other structures. Many evergreen trees

FLOWERS TO GROW FOR AN EVERBLOOMING, COLORFUL GARDEN

These plants will give you some overlap through the seasons for extended color.

Spring-Blooming	Summer-Blooming	Fall-Blooming
Tulip	Echinacea	Sedum 'Autumn Joy'
Daffodil	Black-eyed Susan	Aster
Allium	Bee balm	Chrysanthemum
Iris	Butterfly weed	Winter pansy
Creeping phlox	Daylily	Ornamental grass
Catmint	Liatris	Beautyberry
Salvia	Moonbeam coreopsis	
Knock-out rose	Joe Pye weed	
Peony	Hydrangea	
Hydrangea	Tall garden phlox	
Lenten rose	Dahlia	

grow very tall and wide. Look for plants that are intended for smaller spaces and grow more slowly, like dwarf Alberta spruces. Always read the plant tag and check maturity size before planting.

PRO TIP: Buy small, young plants so they are easier to manage and grow. They cost significantly less, and if the plant doesn't survive, you didn't spend ten times the price.

Cottage Garden Design

Cottage gardens are unique, beautiful, and fun to grow. They afford an opportunity to experiment with different flowers in a forgiving way because they lack a formal structure, making it much easier to manage your garden.

With less focus on spacing or height graduations, there's more emphasis on blending flowers with different colors, textures, and fragrances. Cottage gardens typically start with a semi-permanent element like an arbor, birdhouse, fencing, or some other type of hardscaping feature. But then that structure is softened and accented with amazingly beautiful blooms.

And that's where the fun begins.

When I started gardening over twenty-five years ago, I wanted a cottage garden that would continuously bloom. I started with a few annuals, progressed to perennials, then tucked in some bulbs, and eventually added flowering shrubs and small trees. My love for cottage-style gardening has been an evolution. And it's been a different experience every year because every season inspires and teaches me something new.

One of the things I love about a cottage garden is the ability to express your personal garden style through flowers and foliage. You can grow what you love and combine colors and textures that are pleasing to you. Some of my best plant combinations happened just by playing around with different colors, textures, and blooms. So, have fun with it!

EASY-CARE COTTAGE GARDEN FLOWERS

Lavender	Rudbeckia	Daisy	Marigold
Iris	Sedum 'Autumn Joy'	Snapdragon	Sunflower
Echinacea	Daylily	Pansy	. . . and so many more!
Peony	Hydrangea	Forget-me-not	

Cottage Garden Designs

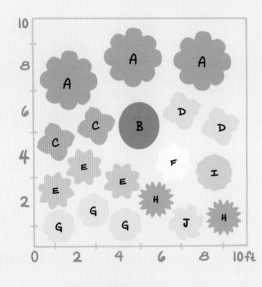

SPRING
A — Baptisia
B — Birdbath
C — Siberian iris
D — Penstemon
E — Salvia 'May Night'
F — Nepeta 'Walker's Low'
G — Myosotis (forget-me-not)
H — Dianthus
I — Peony
J — Pansy

SUMMER
A — Russian sage 'Denim 'n Lace'
B — Birdhouse
C — Clematis 'Jackmanii'
D — Shasta daisy
E — Echinacea
F — Rudbeckia
G — Nepeta 'Walker's Low'
H — 'Supertunia Vista Bubblegum'

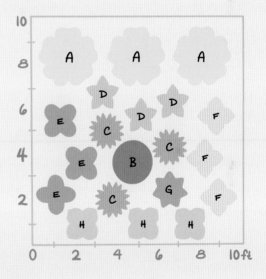

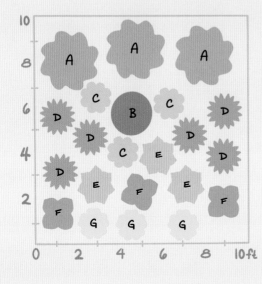

FALL
A — Eupatorium (Joe Pye weed)
B — Obelisk 2' wide
C — Sweet autumn clematis
   (to climb the obelisk)
D — Japanese anenome
E — Sedum 'Autumn Joy'
F — Aster
G — Pansy

The biggest advantage of growing a cottage garden is that it does not need to be perfectly maintained like a formal garden. Flowers are organized in a haphazard sort of way that just works. Cottage gardens also disguise little imperfections because they are imperfectly perfect. And that's the way I love to garden.

Five Quick Ways to Grow a Cottage Garden

1. Start with a small garden and expand it as you gain experience.

2. Begin with structural plants like small evergreens and flowering shrubs and trees.

3. Add a focal point to plant around, such as a birdbath, birdhouse, arbor, bench, chair, fence, path, or other hardscaping element.

4. Plant flowers in groupings with lots of color, texture, dimension, and different bloom times.

5. Repeat plant types and colors for a natural visual flow throughout the bed.

Attracting Butterflies and Hummingbirds

If you want to attract more butterflies and hummingbirds to your garden, realize that some flowering plants entice them more than others. Thankfully, there are a lot of plants that overlap to attract both butterflies and hummingbirds.

How to Grow a Butterfly Garden

If you want to attract butterflies to your garden, a little preplanning can go a long way in helping you grow the right plants and flowers that invite them into your landscape. Butterfly gardens are easy to grow and maintain, since most recommended butterfly-attracting plants are native or easy-care.

Do your research, site your butterfly garden well, and include plants that feed adult butterflies with nectar plants and their caterpillars with host plants. Ideally, you want to select plants that will attract butterflies common to your area.

Location

Most butterfly-loving plants need full sun. And it's recommended to grow nectar plants near fences, shrubs, trees, and vines to provide butterflies with shelter from the wind and rain.

Offer Host Plants

Butterflies lay eggs on certain plants that feed their caterpillars. Thus, butterflies visit gardens with nearby host plants, such as:

- Milkweed
- Viburnum
- Wisteria
- Flowering dogwood
- Snapdragon
- Foxglove

PRO TIP: Instead of cutting back plants during their growing season, let them die back naturally. If you can, wait until early spring to clean up your garden beds because dead plants may contain eggs or developing butterflies on them. While a yard full of dead plants might not look great, it helps keep the butterfly life cycle going.

Provide Nectar Plants

By selecting nectar plants with varying bloom times, butterflies will visit your garden often and will hang around for longer periods of time.

Butterfly-Attracting Garden Designs

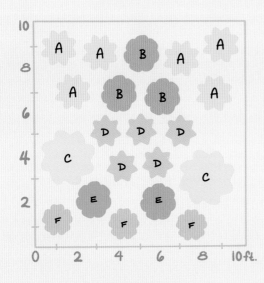

COLORFUL GARDEN
A—Agastache
B—Coneflower
C—Tall Phlox
D—Liatris
E—Nepeta
F—Coreopsis

PINK GARDEN
A—Weigela 'Wine and Roses'
B—Eupatorium (Joe Pye weed)
C—Monarda
D—Zinnia 'Benary's Giant Wine'
E—Sedum 'Autumn's Joy'
F—Dianthus

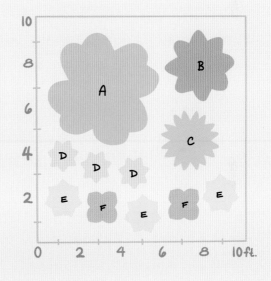

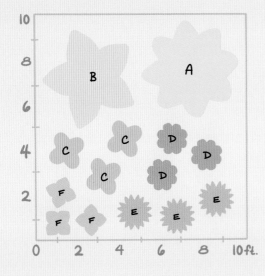

BLUE/PURPLE GARDEN
A—Lilac 'Bloomerang'
B—Rose of Sharon 'Purple Pillar'
C—Agastache
D—Coneflower
E—Salvia 'May Night'
F—Hemerocallis 'Purple De Oro'

Butterfly Garden Quick Tips

- Butterflies favor native plants.

- Avoid both synthetic and homemade pesticides in your garden because they can wipe out butterflies and other pollinators.

- Butterflies are drawn to brightly colored purples, blues, yellows, whites, and pinks.

- Create a succession of flowers that bloom spring through fall to keep butterflies coming back throughout the growing season.

- Butterflies are attracted to clusters of like colors, so plant groupings of the same flowers together.

- Focus on plants with multiple florets and composite flowers because they allow butterflies to get more nectar at one time.

- Avoid double-flowering varieties because they carry less nectar.

How to Grow a Hummingbird Garden

Designing a garden that attracts hummingbirds is very similar to designing a butterfly garden, with some slight nuances.

- Plant a variety of flowers and shrubs in varying heights to provide shade, shelter, food, and water.

- Hummingbirds love brightly colored, tubular flowers because they hold more nectar. Hummingbirds are also drawn to red, orange, pink, and yellow hues.

- Attract hummingbirds to your garden with early blooming varieties so they begin to visit early in the growing season.

❋ Grow similar flowers together in large groupings so hummingbirds can spot them more easily while flying.

EASY-CARE HUMMINGBIRD-ATTRACTING FLOWERS

Nepeta	Echinacea	Columbine	Petunia	Weigela
Bee balm	Cleome	Impatiens	Hibiscus	Hosta

Additional Feeders

Hummingbirds also appreciate artificial feeders filled with nectar to supplement flower nectar. If you choose to use artificial hummingbird feeders, they must be maintained so they don't grow mold or other bacteria, particularly during warmer months.

Simple Hummingbird Feeder Recipe

Mix 4 parts boiled water with 1 part sugar until the sugar dissolves and the solution is clear. You don't need to add red dye. Allow the mixture to cool to room temperature before adding it to a feeder. Clean and replace with a fresh batch every 3 to 4 days.

Deer in the Garden

Deer-Proofing Your Garden

Deer are a huge problem for gardeners in many parts of the country. While no method is foolproof, there are a few precautions we can take to deter deer or at least minimize the damage. Here is a cheat sheet to help you deer-proof your garden.

❋ **Plant smart.** Consult the Rutgers Cooperative Extension list for plants, trees, and shrubs rated by deer resistance: https://njaes.rutgers.edu /deer-resistant-plants/.

Hummingbird-Attracting Designs

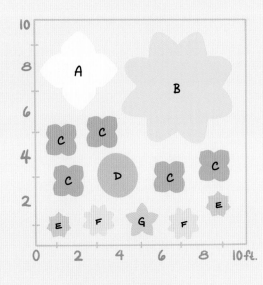

COLORFUL GARDEN
A—Monarda
B—Hardy hibiscus
C—Coneflower
D—Birdbath
E—Daylily
F—Nepeta
G—Petunia

PINK GARDEN
A—Wine and Roses weigela
B—Monarda
C—Salvia 'Pink Profusion'
D—Coneflower
E—Cleome
F—'Supertunia Vista Bubblegum'
G—Achillea 'Firefly Amethyst'

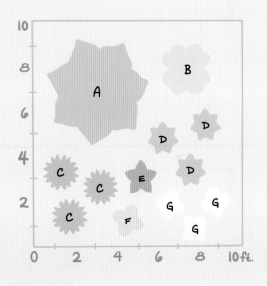

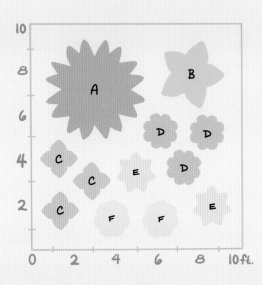

BLUE/PURPLE GARDEN
A—Bloomerang lilac
B—Caryopteris 'Longwood Blue'
C—Salvia 'May Night'
D—Agastache 'Blue Fortune'
E—Nepeta 'Walker's Low'
F—'Supertunia Latte'

- **Use combination plantings.** When planting higher risk plants, group them with plants that are less risky.

- **Spray susceptible plants** with deer repellent, such as Deer Out.

- **Install fencing** that is at least eight feet high.

- **Use scare tactic devices** with motion sensors to frighten them out of your yard.

- **Get a dog.**

- **Walk your gardens daily** to watch for browsing.

- **Prepare in early spring** so you are ready to deal with deer damage before it gets out of control.

EASY-TO-GROW, DEER-RESISTANT COTTAGE GARDEN FLOWERS THAT ATTRACT BUTTERFLIES

Agastache	Lamb's ear	Iris
Nepeta	Peony	Marigold
Allium	Russian sage	Strawflower
Forget-me-not	Globe thistle	Flowering tobacco
Daffodil	Statice	Larkspur
Bleeding heart	Ligularia	Snapdragon
Salvia	Oregano	Cleome
Lavender	False indigo	Rosemary

Deer-Resistant Garden Designs

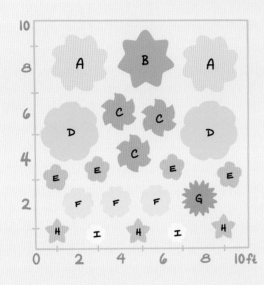

COLORFUL FULL-SUN GARDEN
A — Monarda
B — Russian sage 'Denim 'n Lace'
C — Cleome
D — Echinops
E — Allium 'Globemaster'
F — Bearded iris
G — Nepeta 'Walker's Low'
H — Sweet alyssum
I — Lantana

SHADE/PART-SHADE GARDEN
A — Ligularia 'Bottle Rocket'
B — Bleeding heart
C — Astilbe
D — Hellebore
E — Lungwort
F — Epimedium

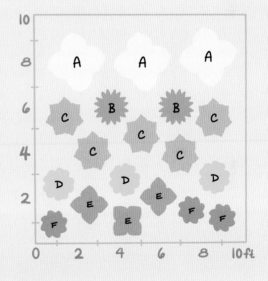

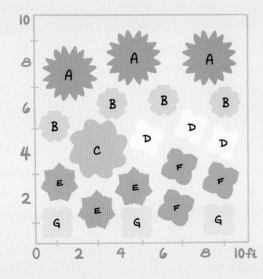

PURPLE FULL-SUN GARDEN
A — Baptisia
B — Allium 'Globemaster'
C — Monarda
D — Bearded iris
E — Lavender 'Hidcote'
F — Salvia 'May Night'
G — Lamb's ear

CHAPTER FOUR

Easy-Care Annuals

If you are just getting started with flower gardening or want to grow your confidence as a gardener, annuals are a great way to get your feet wet. As you gain experience learning what works best for you, your lifestyle, and your garden's growing conditions, you'll start being able to use annuals with more purpose.

In general, annuals complete their whole life cycle within one year. From seed to flower, these plants live and die annually. For this reason, a frost can totally kill them off and they won't return. They are typically planted in spring or fall.

There are some annuals, like celosia and cleome, that drop seeds and can regrow the following year. Some annuals, like chrysanthemums and pansies, thrive in cooler temperatures, while others, like marigolds and petunias, love warmer temperatures. Choose annuals according to the season and your planting purpose.

Using Annuals with More Purpose

Planting annuals helps keep the garden colorful throughout the growing season while bulbs, perennials, and shrubs go through their bloom cycles. Because gardens fade while these plants transition, annuals fill in the gaps with abundantly beautiful flowers, color, and foliage.

They can be grown in mixed borders, planters, hanging baskets, and even in centerpieces on your outdoor dining table. Annuals also play a key role in seasonally decorating the garden. In the spring, you'll notice more pastel-toned annual flowers. In late summer to fall, you'll see more annuals with autumnal hues.

You can also plant annuals to help hide perennial and bulb foliage that has died back during the growing season. This method works really well and helps you avoid cutting back plants too early in case there are developing caterpillar eggs on them or bulbs that need to store energy for the following season's flowers (see chapter 6).

How to Grow Annuals

If plants are not hardy to your zone, they are considered annuals. In general, we plant annuals with that last frost date in mind because annuals that are not cold tolerant can't go in the ground until the threat of frost has passed.

That's not to say you can't plant annuals sooner, but you'll need to throw a frost blanket or sheet over them or move a container of them indoors if a frost is forecasted. So, if you prefer to plant sooner, watch the weather like a hawk and be prepared to protect those tender plants.

When purchasing annuals, timing is everything. For example, don't buy pansies in late spring because they won't survive the summer heat. It's actually better to purchase and plant them in the fall because they are cold-tolerant, can go dormant in the winter, and will bounce back in the spring, depending on your zone. Thus, you can get two seasons out of them instead of just one.

Another example is chrysanthemums. They are beautiful plants for the fall garden, but they're not bred to bloom for more than a few weeks. So, plant them when you want a pop of fall color versus when they first arrive at the nursery in late summer. It's just too hot for them at that time—they'll dry out more quickly, and you'll feel like a gardening failure. Unless you want them at a specific time when you're hosting a party, avoid buying chrysanthemums too early. I know the temptation is strong when you first see them, but wait for at least another month.

Caring for Annuals

Many annuals are super easy to care for. Fertilize them and keep them well-watered during the growing season, and you'll get an abundance of big, beautiful blooms. If you grow annuals in containers, it is even more important to make sure they are fed because every time you water, nutrients wash out of the soil.

Keep annual plants hydrated, particularly during the hot summer months. If you plant annuals in containers or hanging baskets, you may be watering them one to two times a day if the temperatures are hot enough. A general rule of thumb is that if plants wilt, they need water. But if you notice soggy soil and a declining plant? They are likely getting too much water.

Several annuals benefit from deadheading (see chapter 2). Vining annuals may need to be cut back to keep their growth in check. And taller annual plants may need additional support so they don't topple over.

If this is your first time growing annuals (or you think you kill things), pay attention to the plants you grow the first year to get a feel for how different plants grow and handle the weather you have throughout the seasons. You can also work with one type of annual plant at a time until you get comfortable with its care, and then add others.

Budget-Friendly Garden Design Tip

When choosing annuals in the spring, think about how those same annuals will look in the fall. Select flowers that do double duty and look amazing during both seasons. This will help you save money in the long run because you won't need to replace spring annuals with fall varieties if the color is still there.

I love marigolds for this very reason. They look great in spring, do well all summer long, are easy to care for, and the color looks incredible as the color palette deepens well into fall.

Favorite Easy-Care, Low-Maintenance Annuals You Should Grow

While this is not an exhaustive list, here are some annuals I plant yearly because they are such easy-care workhorses in the garden.

Marigold

Marigolds are easygoing flowers that add steady color with an abundance of blooms in the changing seasons. They are almost completely pest- and disease-free but require some deadheading to keep them looking pretty. When planted among vegetables, they make great companion plants that draw pests away from certain plants. Deer tend to leave them alone too.

*Favorite varieties include 'Queen Sophia' and 'Giant Yellow'.

Common Name marigold

Botanical Name *Tagetes*

Plant Family Asteraceae

USDA Hardiness Zones 2–11

Soil Type well-drained, moist, occasionally dry

Soil pH acidic, alkaline, neutral

Sun Exposure full sun

Mature Plant Size height: 12 to 48 inches; width: 6 to 12 inches

Bloom Time summer

Flower Color gold, yellow, orange

Native Area Mexico, Central/South America

Petunia

Petunias are prolific bloomers that are relatively deer-resistant, grow quickly, and look amazing when planted in the front of a mixed border, along pathways, in containers, or in hanging baskets. Deadhead and cut back untidy growth as needed, keep them fertilized, and you'll be rewarded with healthy flowers from spring until the first frost.

*Favorite varieties include Proven Winners 'Supertunia Vista Bubblegum' and Proven Winners 'Supertunia Latte'.

Common Name petunia

Botanical Name
Petunia × hybrida

Plant Family Solanaceae

USDA Hardiness Zones
10a, 10b, 11a, 11b

Soil Type well-drained, moist

Soil pH 6.0–7.0

Sun Exposure full sun, partial shade

Mature Plant Size
height: 6 to 18 inches; width: 12 to 36 inches

Bloom Time summer

Flower Color
blue, gold, green, orange, pink, purple, red, variegated, white

Native Area South America

Celosia

Celosia comes in a variety of colors with different types of textured blooms. They are easy to start from seed and make wonderful cut flowers for arrangements. They reseed well on their own where I live and have returned the following growing season. Celosia looks best in summer through fall, so choose color options that will carry you through the full growing season.

*Favorite varieties include 'Pink Champagne' and 'Coral Reef'.

Common Name celosia

Botanical Name *Celosia*

Plant Family Amaranthaceae

USDA Hardiness Zones
10b, 10a, 11b, 11a

Soil Type well-drained, high in organic matter

Soil pH neutral

Sun Exposure full sun

Mature Plant Size
height: 6 to 36 inches; width: 16 to 18 inches

Bloom Time summer

Flower Color
gold, orange, pink, red, white

Native Area Africa

Pansy

Pansies are one of the first annuals you'll find at nurseries in early spring. They grow quickly with heart-like blooms that complement spring-flowering bulbs and fall garden mums. Pansies are cold-tolerant in both spring and fall, but will die in the summer heat. Plant them in pots or in the front of mixed borders and pathways. Critters like deer and rabbits like to eat pansies, so they'll need protection from wildlife.

*Favorite varieties include 'Frizzle Sizzle' and 'Nature Mulberry Shades'.

Common Name pansy

Botanical Name
Viola × wittrockiana

Plant Family Violaceae

USDA Hardiness Zones
7–11

Soil Type well-drained

Soil pH
slightly acidic (6.0–6.2), neutral

Sun Exposure
full sun, partial shade

Mature Plant Size
height: 4 to 8 inches; width:
4 to 6 inches

Bloom Time
spring, summer, fall

Flower Color
blue, cream, gold, orange,
purple, variegated, white

Native Area Europe, Asia

Impatiens

Impatiens were the very first flower I grew, and you can't beat them for planting in shadier spots. They grow well both in containers and when planted in the ground, and they come in a variety of colors that mix well with coleus, sweet potato vines, and baby's-breath euphorbia. Impatiens are fast growers, but they are not deer-resistant and need protection from wildlife.

*Favorite varieties include Proven Winners 'Rockapulco Purple' and Proven Winners 'Rockapulco Appleblossom'.

Common Name
impatiens, garden balsam

Botanical Name
Impatiens balsamina

Plant Family Balsaminaceae

USDA Hardiness Zones
2–11

Soil Type well-drained, moist

Soil pH acidic, alkaline, neutral

Sun Exposure
full sun, partial shade

Mature Plant Size
height: 6 to 30 inches; width:
6 to 18 inches

Bloom Time
fall, spring, summer

Flower Color
pink, purple, red, white

Native Area
Western/Southern India

Zinnia

Zinnias are my favorite annual to start from seed because they grow quickly, come in an array of beautiful colors, and provide you with wonderful cut flowers. While you can find some varieties at the nursery, there are *so* many more options if you start them from seed. Whether you start them indoors or direct sow them in the garden, zinnia seeds germinate with ease and are a great option if you've never before started plants from seed. Taller varieties may require staking. These prolific bloomers are cut and come again, so don't be shy about enjoying them in a vase.

*Favorite varieties include 'Benary's Giant Wine' and 'Queen Lime Blush'.

Common Name zinnia

Botanical Name *Zinnia*

Plant Family Asteraceae

USDA Hardiness Zones
3–10

Soil Type
moist, occasionally dry

Soil pH acidic, alkaline, neutral

Sun Exposure full sun

Mature Plant Size
height: 8 to 48 inches; width:
6 to 18 inches

Bloom Time
fall, spring, summer

Flower Color
gold, orange, pink, purple, red,
variegated, white

Native Area South America

Nasturtium

Nasturtiums are fun to grow and come in an array of rich colors with bushy, trailing, and climbing varieties. The flowers and foliage are edible with a peppery flavor, and nasturtiums can be used in vegetable gardens as companion plants to help keep pests at bay. While nasturtiums can easily be started by seed indoors, they direct sow well too.

*Favorite varieties include 'Alaska Mix' and 'Jewel Mix'.

Common Name
common nasturtium

Botanical Name
Tropaeolum majus

Plant Family Tropaeolaceae

USDA Hardiness Zones
2–11

Soil Type loamy, sandy, well-drained

Soil pH acidic, alkaline, neutral

Sun Exposure
full sun, partial sun

Mature Plant Size
height: 12 inches (bush) to 10 feet (climbing vine); width: 12 to 36 inches

Bloom Time fall, spring, summer

Flower Color gold, orange, pink, red, white

Native Area
Central/South America

Baby's-Breath Euphorbia

Baby's-breath euphorbia (not to be confused with the baby's breath *Gypsophila* you may know from the florist) is a great filler plant that has an airy appearance and weaves among other plants as it grows. If you see this plant at the nursery, buy several. It grows quickly, looks amazing from spring to fall with no deadheading necessary, and deer tend to leave it alone. Baby's-breath euphorbia looks incredible in containers and in mixed borders with its billowy clusters of flowers.

*Favorite varieties include Proven Winners Euphorbia 'Diamond Frost' and Proven Winners Euphorbia 'Diamond Mountain'.

Common Name baby's-breath euphorbia, graceful spurge

Botanical Name *Euphorbia hypericifolia*

Plant Family Euphorbiaceae

USDA Hardiness Zones 10–11

Soil Type Loamy, well-drained

Soil pH Neutral to acidic

Sun Exposure full sun, partial shade

Mature Plant Size height: 12 to 18 inches; width: 12 to 24 inches

Bloom Time late spring, summer

Flower Color white

Native Area North America

Bacopa

Bacopa is the perfect plant for container gardens or hanging baskets because it spills beautifully over the sides and blooms like crazy if you treat it right. Keep it fertilized and moist so it keeps producing during hot summers.

*Favorite varieties include Proven Winners 'Snowstorm Giant Snowflake' and Proven Winners 'Snowstorm Blue'.

Common Name bacopa

Botanical Name
Chaenostoma cordatum

Plant Family
Scrophulariaceae

USDA Hardiness Zones
9–11

Soil Type occasionally dry

Soil pH acidic

Sun Exposure partial shade

Mature Plant Size height:
3 to 6 inches; width: 12 to 24
inches

Bloom Time fall, summer

Flower Color purple, lavender,
white

Native Area Southern Africa

Sunflower

Is there a happier bloom than a sunflower? I love to start them from seed every year because they are easy to germinate and fun to grow. Direct sow sunflower seeds after all danger of frost has passed and let them do the rest in mid-to-late summer. In some cases, they'll need staking, but otherwise you just let them do their thing and enjoy!

*Favorite varieties include 'Panache' and 'Royal Hybrid'.

Common Name sunflower

Botanical Name *Helianthus annuus*

Plant Family Asteraceae

USDA Hardiness Zones 2–11

Soil Type well-drained, sandy, loamy, clay

Soil pH acidic, 6.0–6.8

Sun Exposure full sun

Mature Plant Size height: 18 inches to 10 feet; width: 18 to 36 inches

Bloom Time fall, summer

Flower Color yellow

Native Area Western United States

Geranium

Sun-loving geraniums bring nonstop color from late spring until fall. They can even be overwintered indoors and replanted again the following season. Geraniums thrive in beds or containers, require minimal care aside from deadheading, and flower with ease.

*Favorite varieties include Proven Winners 'Boldly Hot Pink' and Proven Winners 'Boldly Lavender Rose'.

Common Name geranium

Botanical Name
Pelargonium × hortorum

Plant Family Geraniaceae

USDA Hardiness Zones
10–11

Soil Type medium moisture

Soil pH 6.0–6.5

Sun Exposure
full sun, partial shade

Mature Plant Size
height: 12 to 24 inches;
width: 6 to 20 inches

Bloom Time mid-May to early
June

Flower Color
pale pink, lavender, red, white

Native Area
Eastern North America

Snapdragon

While you can find snapdragon flowers at the nursery, it's best to start these plants from seed because there are so many more gorgeous varieties to choose from. Shorter varieties require less work than larger ones that may need staking. Snapdragons are deer-resistant, make incredible cut flowers, and give all the cottage garden feels during the growing season. Since they thrive in cooler temperatures, they slow down flower production in summer. But leave them be, as they can bounce back and bloom again in the fall.

*Favorite varieties include 'Madame Butterfly Bronze with White' and 'Costa Apricot'.

Common Name snapdragon

Botanical Name
Antirrhinum majus

Plant Family Plantaginaceae

USDA Hardiness Zones
7–10

Soil Type well-drained, high in organic matter

Soil pH slightly acidic

Sun Exposure
full sun, partial shade

Mature Plant Size
height: 6 to 36 inches;
width: 6 to 18 inches

Bloom Time
fall, spring, summer

Flower Color gold, orange, pink, purple, white, lavender

Native Area
Southwestern Europe

While I can go on and on about my favorite easy-care annuals to grow, I suggest starting with a variety or two listed above if you want to gain some experience growing flowers with success. Annuals are a great starting point for beginners because they are generally less expensive than other types of plants. So you can learn as you grow while easily changing up your garden's look from year to year without making a large investment. Not to mention, they look amazing throughout the growing season and grow well in planters, making them perfect for smaller spaces.

ANNUAL PLANTS THAT LOOK GOOD TOGETHER

Shade/Part Shade—Coleus, sweet potato vine, and double flowering impatiens

Part Shade—Coleus, bacopa, sweet potato vine, and begonia

Full Sun—Geranium, baby's-breath euphorbia, petunia, and bacopa

Full Sun—Marigold, baby's-breath euphorbia, petunia, and lantana

Full Sun—Zinnia, snapdragon, and petunia

Sun, Fall Flowering—Chrysanthemum, pansy, and celosia

Sun, Spring Flowering—Pansy, ranunculus, and licorice plant

CHAPTER FIVE

Winning Perennials

If you want to start growing plants that require minimal maintenance year to year, perennials are a great option. In the first year, you'll plant and take care of them. If they like your garden, they'll return the following season with little to no work from you.

Perennials are plants that live more than two years. They're typically cold-hardy plants that die back and regrow the following growing season. Some perennials can live a really long time while others may peter out after a few seasons.

If you find a few easy-care perennial plants with different bloom times throughout the growing season, you'll have a garden that constantly flowers and changes without you having to do a whole lot of work. Easy-care perennials are also more disease-resistant, have long-lasting blooms, and look good for extended periods of time. These plants don't require staking or pesticides, and they don't need to be coddled to become well-established in your garden.

Sounds like a win, right?

Perennials do well both in the ground and planted in containers. They'll only last a few years in a container, though, so you'll need to transplant them to the ground or repot them with fresh soil if you want to keep them alive after a year or two. If you repot a plant, try to gently remove as much soil from the root ball as you can, and then repot it with fresh soil. Depending on your hardiness zone, it may be easier to treat a perennial like an annual and replace it yearly so it's a little less work.

To overwinter them outdoors, choose perennials that are two zones hardier than your zone and plant them in a weather-resistant container that will not break from freezing and thawing. It is best to leave them outside, but planters can be moved to an unheated garage or shed during harsh cold months to protect the perennials from winter damage.

Note that some perennials, like peonies, need time to establish a strong root system and may not bloom the first year or two. If they have been recently planted and otherwise look healthy, just be patient and trust that they'll eventually flower.

How to Grow Perennials

Your hardiness zone determines what is perennial to your locality. Unless they are planted in containers, perennials don't need to be fertilized. Just make sure they have good-quality soil.

Because perennials grow, bloom, and die back, they may need to be pruned or cut back during the season to neaten up the garden or to promote more flowering. Thus, some perennials are more work than others, so do some research before you grow.

Dividing Perennials

For the most part, perennials don't need much to do their thing. But every few years after planting, they need to be divided to keep them looking good. And while that sounds like a lot of work, it's not hard—and you'll have extras to plant in other areas of the garden or to give away to friends.

We divide plants to:

* Keep them healthy

* Control their growth and overall size

- Avoid overcrowding, which leads to fewer or smaller blooms due to plants receiving fewer nutrients, light, or air circulation

- Expand the garden in a budget-friendly way

- Keep aggressive plants under control

How to Divide Perennials

1. Determine where the natural lines of division are. Some plants will show signs of separating themselves and others will not. In the latter case, you'll need to make the decision where to divide the plant.

2. With a spade shovel, start with the plant's outer edge. Dig underneath the plant, making sure to avoid slicing the roots as much as possible. Some plants will lift easily with one simple dig and the use of your hands. Others will require more effort and you'll need to dig around the entire section of the plant.

3. Use your spade or garden fork to gently separate the clump into smaller sections, making sure each section has a good portion of roots and shoots. How many sections you make largely depends on the plant's size and natural divisions.

4. Don't worry about injuring plants during this process. They will regenerate and bounce back.

5. Once the divisions have been made, replant the sections as soon as possible.

When to Divide Perennials

You'll know that perennials need to be divided when they stop producing as many flowers as they used to, or in many cases, you'll see the plant almost

dividing itself, creating a sort of hole in the middle. You also might have perennials that love your garden so much that they start taking over an area and crowding out other plants.

It's best to divide perennials in the spring or fall when the weather is cooler and the plants are either breaking ground or going dormant. They are easier to establish this way and require little to no work from you. I strongly recommend that you avoid dividing and transplanting perennials in the summer. While it can be done, it's more work, and the success rate is very low.

Cooler temperatures provide a better environment for success because transplants don't need as much coddling to reacclimate. It's more work to establish transplants when it's hot out because you'll actively need to keep them hydrated and possibly shaded.

I divide perennials in early spring or mid-to-late fall when it's much cooler and the plants can basically take care of themselves. If I don't get a chance to divide them in the early spring, I will wait until those plants start to go dormant in mid-to-late fall, when I don't care what the plants will look like after I divide them.

Another benefit to dividing perennials in the fall is that the plants have time to grow stronger root systems over the winter instead of stressing through a hot summer.

My Favorite Easy-Care, Low-Maintenance Perennials

I had a really hard time narrowing down this list because there are so many great options to grow! I probably have more than fifty favorite perennials, but I couldn't fit them all in this book.

Hellebore

Lenten rose is a deer-resistant perennial that flowers in late winter with an extended bloom time. It grows gorgeous, leather-like evergreen leaves, has the prettiest flowers, and is a must-have for any shade garden.

*Favorite varieties include Proven Winners Wedding Party 'Wedding Crasher' and Proven Winners Wedding Party 'Dashing Groomsmen'.

Common Name Lenten rose, hellebore, Christmas rose

Botanical Name
Helleborus orientalis

Plant Family Ranunculaceae

USDA Hardiness Zones 4–9

Soil Type moist, well-drained, loamy, sandy

Soil pH neutral, alkaline

Sun Exposure dappled sunlight, deep shade, partial shade

Mature Plant Size
height: 12 to 18 inches;
width: 12 to 18 inches

Bloom Time spring, winter

Flower Color cream, pink, purple, red, white

Native Area Asia Minor, Eurasia

Dicentra

Dicentra is one of my favorite deer-resistant, easy-care flowering plants for shade with its pretty, heart-shaped flowers that bloom in the spring. Plant it in the middle to the back of the border so when it dies back in early summer, you won't see the yellowing foliage or gaping hole it leaves behind.

*Favorite varieties include Dicentra Spectabilis 'Alba' and Proven Winners 'Pink Diamonds'.

Common Name
bleeding heart

Botanical Name
Dicentra spectabilis

Plant Family Fumariaceae

USDA Hardiness Zones 3–9

Soil Type well-drained, damp

Soil pH alkaline, neutral

Sun Exposure partial shade

Mature Plant Size
height: 17 to 48 inches;
width: 12 to 24 inches

Bloom Time late spring,
early summer

Flower Color white, pink

Native Area Japan, China,
Korea, Siberia

Nepeta

Nepeta is a must-have, deer-resistant plant with minimal pest or disease problems and long-lasting blooms. It billows with pretty, hummingbird-attracting tubular flower spikes on fragrant silvery gray foliage. If you cut it back halfway after the first set of blooms fade, you can encourage a second set of flowers. As a small- to medium-sized perennial, nepeta is a great plant for edging gardens and lining pathways. I also love it paired with roses.

*Favorite varieties include 'Walker's Low' and 'Cat's Pajamas'.

Common Name catmint

Botanical Name *Nepeta*

Plant Family Lamiaceae

USDA Hardiness Zones 3–8

Soil Type
clay, loamy, sandy, rocky

Soil pH acidic, alkaline, neutral

Sun Exposure full sun

Mature Plant Size
height: 12 to 24 inches;
width: 12 to 24 inches

Bloom Time spring, summer

Flower Color
blue, purple, white

Native Area Temperate
Eurasia, Macaronesia,
Eastern Tropical Africa

Salvia

Salvias are deer-resistant perennials with an extended bloom time that are relatively pest- and disease-free. If you cut them back halfway after the first set of blooms, you can encourage a second set of flowers. As a medium-sized plant, they do well in the front or middle of the border and look best when planted in groupings.

*Favorite varieties include 'May Night' and Proven Winners Color Spires 'Crystal Blue'.

Common Name
common sage

Botanical Name
Salvia officinalis

Plant Family Lamiaceae

USDA Hardiness Zones 4–8

Soil Type
free-draining, medium-dry

Soil pH 6–7

Sun Exposure full sun

Mature Plant Size
height: 24 inches;
width: 24 to 36 inches

Bloom Time spring, summer

Flower Color
blue-lavender, pink-lavender

Native Area Mediterranean

Astilbe

Astilbes are medium-sized, deer-resistant perennials that produce beautiful, showy flowers that add lots of color, texture, and dimension to shadier spots. With fernlike foliage, they come in many colors and look best planted in the front to middle of borders.

*Favorite varieties include 'Fanal' and 'Peach Blossom'.

Common Name astilbe

Botanical Name
Astilbe japonica

Plant Family Saxifragaceae

USDA Hardiness Zones 4–9

Soil Type moist, loamy

Soil pH acidic, alkaline

Sun Exposure
dappled sunlight, deep shade, partial shade

Mature Plant Size
height: 12 to 48 inches;
width: 12 to 24 inches

Bloom Time spring, summer

Flower Color pink, white, red

Native Area Japan, China

Bearded Iris

Bearded irises are gorgeous flowers that resist deer and are relatively pest- and disease-free. The petals are truly striking, with an ombre appearance and a wide array of colors. Plant reblooming or several different varieties in garden beds to extend their bloom time. Some iris varieties grow quite tall and may need staking.

*Favorite varieties include 'Recurring Delight' and 'Angel's Rest'.

Common Name bearded iris

Botanical Name
Iris × germanica

Plant Family Iridaceae

USDA Hardiness Zones 3–9

Soil Type well-drained, occasionally dry, very dry

Soil pH 6–7.5

Sun Exposure
full sun, partial shade

Maturity Height and Width
height: 12 to 48 inches;
width: 12 to 24 inches

Bloom Time summer

Flower Color black, blue, cream, gold, orange, pink, purple, red, white, variegated

Native Area Mediterranean

Lavender

A well-loved perennial, lavender is a beautiful, deer-resistant plant with silvery gray-green foliage, purple flower spikes, and a fragrance you can't beat. Its compact shrub form and medium-sized growing habit look pretty situated near the front or in the middle of a mixed border, but lavender does well in containers too. It thrives in full sun and drier conditions.

*Favorite varieties include 'Munstead' and 'Hidcote'.

Common Name lavender

Botanical Name
Lavandula angustifolia

Plant Family Lamiaceae

USDA Hardiness Zones 5–9

Soil Type well-drained, light

Soil PH 6.1–8.2

Sun Exposure full sun

Maturity Height and Width
height: 12 to 36 inches;
width: 24 to 48 inches

Bloom Time
early-to-late summer

Flower Color violet, pink

Native Area
France, Italy, Spain

Coreopsis

Coreopsis is a mounding, deer-resistant perennial with masses of bright and dainty flowers. It is easy-care, low-maintenance, drought-tolerant, and has long-lasting blooms. Plant coreopsis along a border or use it to fill in a bed with fun pops of color.

Favorite Varieties include 'Moonbeam' and 'Creme Caramel'.

Common Name
common coreopsis,
large-flower tickseed

Botanical Name
Coreopsis grandiflora

Plant Family Asteraceae

USDA Hardiness Zones 4–9

Soil Type
well-drained, dry, sandy, rocky

Soil pH acidic, neutral

Sun Exposure partial shade

Mature Plant Size
height: 12 to 36 inches;
width: 12 to 36 inches

Bloom Time spring, summer

Flower Color yellow

Native Area Canada, USA

Hosta

Hostas might be one of the easiest perennials to grow because they thrive in full shade, can tolerate some sun, and create great visual impact in the garden. They grow well in containers and produce pretty tubular flowers in the summer that can attract hummingbirds. With very striking foliage, hostas come in a variety of shapes, colors, and sizes. They do need protection from deer.

*Favorite varieties include 'Blueberry Muffin' and Proven Winners Shadowland 'Echo the Sun'.

Common Name hosta

Botanical Name *Hosta*

Plant Family Asparagaceae

USDA Hardiness Zones 3–9

Soil Type well-drained, high in organic matter

Soil PH 6.5–7.5

Sun Exposure deep shade, partial shade

Mature Plant Size height: 18 to 30 inches; width: 12 to 36 inches

Bloom Time summer

Flower Color lavender, white

Native Area Asia

Hemerocallis

Daylilies are great starter plants for new gardeners, as these colorful, carefree flowers grow quickly with ease. They can handle most types of soil, love summer heat, and have minimal pest and disease problems. While they are easy to grow, deer will decimate them if given the chance, so they do need protection.

*Favorite varieties include 'Frosted Vintage Ruffles' and 'Bettylen'.

Common Name daylily

Botanical Name *Hemerocallis*

Plant Family
Hemerocallidaceae

USDA Hardiness Zones 3–9

Soil Type well-drained,
high in organic matter

Soil pH 6–6.5

Sun Exposure
full sun, partial shade

Mature Plant Size
height: 12 to 36 inches;
width: 12 to 36 inches

Bloom Time
late spring to early fall

Flower Color gold, orange,
pink, purple, red, white

Native Area Asia

Echinacea

Coneflowers come in lots of different varieties, sizes, and colors, so there's a type for every garden. Echinacea is drought-tolerant, has an extended bloom time, and self-sows with ease. It's also a pollinator magnet, but I've found the foliage to be susceptible to deer damage and may require protection. Plant taller varieties of echinacea in the back of the border and give it plenty of room to grow.

*Favorite varieties include Echinacea Purpurea 'Magnus' and Proven Winners Double Coded 'Raspberry Beret'.

Common Name
purple coneflower

Botanical Name *Echinacea purpurea*

Plant Family Asteraceae

USDA Hardiness Zones 3–8

Soil Type
well-drained, moist, loamy

Soil pH neutral

Sun Exposure
full sun, partial shade

Mature Plant Size
height: 36 to 48 inches;
width: 12 to 24 inches

Bloom Time
summer to mid-fall

Flower Color pinkish-purple

Native Area
Eastern/Central USA

Rudbeckia

Rudbeckia is one of the first perennials I grew and loved because it grows with ease and has very few problems. Depending on the variety, it starts flowering in the summer and blooms well into the fall. Rudbeckia looks best when planted in the middle to the back of the border. Deer sometimes browse it, though, so it may need protection in some areas.

*Favorite varieties include 'American Gold Rush' and 'Goldsturm'.

Common Name
black-eyed Susan

Botanical Name
Rudbeckia hirta

Plant Family Asteraceae

USDA Hardiness Zones 3–8

Soil Type well-drained, clay, loamy, sandy

Soil pH acidic, alkaline, neutral

Sun Exposure
sun, partial shade

Mature Plant Size
height: 24 to 48 inches;
width: 12 to 24 inches

Bloom Time summer, fall

Flower Color gold

Native Area Eastern USA

Sedum 'Autumn Joy'

While there are different varieties of sedum to grow, Sedum 'Autumn Joy' is one of my favorite perennials to grow because it's enjoyable throughout the year. In spring, the foliage adds interest while the plant grows. It doesn't truly bloom until late summer to early fall, but you can't beat the texture from the chartreuse-colored flower heads that appear before they open and go from a light pink blossom to a much deeper red in autumn. After the flowers fade and dry out, they look great in winter planters or left in the garden covered with snow. This fuss-free flower works well when planted in the front or middle of the garden. Deer may browse it, so give it some protection.

Common Name
sedum 'Autumn Joy'

Botanical Name
Hylotelephium

Plant Family Crassulaceae

USDA Hardiness Zones
3–10

Soil Type
well-drained, gravelly

Soil pH 5.6–6, slightly acidic

Sun Exposure full sun,
morning/afternoon shade

Mature Plant Size
height: 12 to 24 inches;
width: 12 to 24 inches

Bloom Time fall, summer

Flower Color pink, orange

Native Area China

Achillea

I have to admit, I never grew yarrow until we moved to our new home in 2021. There's no particular reason why, I just didn't. When I started my new gardens at the house I live in now, I planted a few varieties—and I love them! Achillea is fuss-free with gorgeous, flat flower heads that provide texture and beautiful blooms all summer long. It is easy to grow, has few pest and disease problems, and fits well in many types of gardens.

*Favorite varieties include 'Firefly Amethyst' and 'Firefly Peach Sky'.

Common Name
common yarrow

Botanical Name
Achillea millefolium

Plant Family Asteraceae

USDA Hardiness Zones 3–9

Soil Type loamy, sandy, occasionally dry, occasionally wet

Soil pH neutral

Sun Exposure full sun

Mature Plant Size
height: 12 to 36 inches;
width: 12 to 46 inches

Bloom Time summer

Flower Color cream, gold, purple, pink, white, orange

Native Area Europe, Western Asia, North America

PERENNIALS THAT LOOK GOOD TOGETHER

Shade—Hosta, astilbe, and hellebore

Part Shade/Shade—Brunnera, hellebore, and Virginia bluebell

Shade with Annuals—Bleeding heart, hosta, astilbe, lungwort, and impatiens

Sun—Echinacea, monarda, Russian sage, Joe Pye weed, and sedum 'Autumn Joy'

Sun—Coreopsis, achillea, echinacea, salvia, and nepeta

Sun—Baptisia, monarda, Russian sage, coneflower, rudbeckia, coreopsis, and lavender

Sun with Annuals—Baptisia, Russian sage, coneflower, rudbeckia, zinnia, and petunia

Since perennials return yearly, they are the perfect option to provide long-lasting color and interest without a whole lot of work. There are many easy-care perennials to choose from that are low-maintenance and simple to grow. While they can be more expensive up front, perennials save you money over time because the investment returns yearly without the need to purchase more new plants every season. If you are looking to create a more budget-friendly, sustainable garden, working with perennials is a great easy-care option.

CHAPTER SIX

Spring-Flowering Bulbs

If you want to see early blooms in the garden, planting spring-flowering bulbs is a must. Without them, gardens will have a prolonged dull and dreary appearance until perennials break through the ground and spring nursery stock is available.

Hardy bulbs, like daffodils and tulips, are a great way to get that early season color before perennials and annuals take over.

But the best part? They grow and bloom while the temperatures are cool, with little to no work from you after you're done planting them.

How to Plant Bulbs in the Fall

Spring-flowering bulbs must be planted in the fall so they have time to develop a good root system before winter sets in and gives them enough of the winter chill that's required for them to bloom in the spring.

It is best to wait to plant your bulbs until soil temperatures are below 60 degrees. Depending on where you live, that means the best time to plant is generally mid-September or October when temperatures are consistently cool.

If you bought or received spring-blooming bulbs like tulips or daffodils as full-grown plants in the spring, you can plant them directly in the ground and they should return the following spring.

Bulbs also do well in containers. Plant them in the fall, lightly water them once, and keep them in an unheated garage or shed through the winter so they are chilled from the weather but don't succumb to the continual freezing and thawing that can rot them out. Move them outdoors as the temperatures warm, usually in March or April, depending on your zone.

How to Buy Bulbs

In general, spring-flowering bulbs are available in the fall from local nurseries or big-box stores. However, there's much more variety if you buy bulbs online. And if you want the best selection, order them in the winter for fall delivery. Regardless of where you buy, always look for bulbs that are large, firm, and have good color.

Some of my favorite online suppliers for bulbs are Johnny's Seeds, Floret Flower Farm, White Flower Farm, Longfield Gardens, and Colorblends.

Designing and Growing a Garden with Bulbs

If you don't have a garden plan and want to just tuck some bulbs into your garden, place them on the ground where you want to plant them to get a general idea of how things will look before you start digging the bulbs in. You can plant them in individual holes or group them together, but try to first have at least a rough idea of how you want things to look.

For a natural, effortless look, many gardeners simply toss bulbs on the ground and plant them where they land. I prefer to plant them in groupings because it is more aesthetically pleasing to the eye when they flower and much easier to plant them in groups instead of digging individual holes for each bulb.

When plants emerge in spring, it's recommended to fertilize them lightly with bulb fertilizer at least two inches from the plant. I don't always do this, so don't worry if you don't either, particularly if you already pay attention to your soil quality.

How to Plant Bulbs in the Fall

SUPPLIES

- bulbs
- shovel
- bulb planter or trowel
- bulb fertilizer
- garden soil
- organic matter like peat moss

DIRECTIONS

1. Choose a garden location that receives at least six hours of sun and has good drainage.
2. Before planting bulbs, place them on top of the bed to plan out your design.
3. Dig holes to the recommended depth. In general, plant bulbs three times as deep as the bulb's greatest dimension. Make sure bulbs are upright with the pointed ends up and root ends down.
4. Before backfilling the hole, add organic matter like peat moss to add drainage and help enrich the soil.
5. Mix in a special bulb fertilizer. Backfill and water well.

WHAT HAPPENS IF YOU PLANT A BULB UPSIDE DOWN?

While it can still grow, a bulb planted upside down will be stressed and might die. The best way to know whether you are planting a bulb correctly is to look for the roots, which are found underneath the wide base. The pointed tip should be planted facing up, as that is where the flower grows.

Wildlife Problems

Avoid using bone meal if rodents, skunks, or other small animals are an issue in your garden, because bone meal attracts them. If you suspect animals are digging up and eating your bulbs, try surrounding the area with chicken wire.

How to Protect Tulips and Other Plants from Deer

While many spring-flowering bulbs are deer-resistant, tulips are not one of them. Deer *love* to eat tulips. If you have deer in your area, your tulips will need protection. We get herds of deer every year, all season long, that would decimate my tulips if I didn't protect them. The following method is very effective if you are aggressive with the application. And it works well with other susceptible plants too.

- Spray deer repellent on plant foliage as soon as the tulip shoot breaks through the ground.

- Spray again when the tulip is about one-third to one-half of its full height.

- Spray again when the tulip forms the flower head but is not open yet.

- Spray one last time when the flower starts to bloom.

- If you're protecting other plants like hosta from deer, continue spraying repellent monthly or every few weeks when the plant is fully mature.

While I can't promise you this method is 100 percent effective—because deer will eat anything if they are hungry enough—it's definitely worth trying on a small patch to see if it makes a difference.

What to Do If Bulbs Don't Bloom

While most hardy bulbs can bloom for decades after they are planted, bulbs that fail to bloom are not uncommon. To evaluate what happened, consider the following to identify what might have impacted flowering and how you can fix it.

- If bulbs were planted in the fall and no blooms or foliage appear in the spring, it's possible that critters like voles or squirrels got to them.

- Did you plant high-quality bulbs? The bigger the bulb, the better the bloom.

- Bulbs should be fed with 5-10-10 fertilizer twice—when they are planted in the fall and after leaves emerge in the spring.

- Test the soil to see if there's too much nitrogen.

- Make sure that lawn fertilizer is not seeping into the area where your bulbs are planted.

- Bulbs need to receive six to eight hours of full sun each day.

- Bulbs might be competing for nutrients with nearby plants that overcrowd or shade them. Relocate the bulbs if needed.

- Check the drainage where bulbs are planted. If the area is retaining too much water, your bulbs will rot.

Design Tip: When the flowers fade, remove the flower parts and stem before the plant goes to seed, but don't cut the leaves back until they turn yellow. This allows the bulb to store more energy for next year's flower production.

- Foliage that is cut back too early in the spring can affect the following year's blooms. Always wait until leaves turn yellow before cutting foliage back. I know it's unsightly, but either plant annuals and perennials around the bulbs to conceal the dieback or fold, tie, or rubber-band the foliage to neaten up its appearance.

Design Tip: To hide bulb foliage that is dying back, plant bulbs between perennials and annuals. This will provide color while perennials emerge, and in turn, the perennials will help camouflage the fading foliage.

- If bulbs were transplanted, they may be stressed from the move and need time to reacclimate. Be patient.

- If bulbs have weak foliage, no flowers, or otherwise don't look so great, they could have a virus, especially if the leaves look streaked or mottled. Dig them up and toss them before the virus spreads to other bulbs in the garden. Do not compost them.

- An unusually wet, cold, or hot and dry year could affect the next year's growth and flowering.

- If they've been in the same place for several years, dig and divide bulbs after the leaves turn yellow in the spring.

If you've considered the above possibilities and still aren't sure what happened to your bulbs, dig them up after the foliage yellows and divide them into individual bulbs. Replant them immediately or wait until the fall. If you replant in the fall, keep the bulbs in a cool, dry spot and store them in a mesh bag or in perlite until replanting them.

Easy-Care Bulbs to Grow

Now that we've covered planting, growing, and caring for spring-flowering bulbs, here are some of my easy-care favorites that I grow in my garden.

Crocus

Crocus are typically the earliest spring-flowering bulbs to bloom. They have deer-resistant flowers and small blooms, and they multiply with ease. You can extend their bloom time by planting different varieties. Plant crocus bulbs at the front of a border or in a small corner of the garden for the greatest impact.

PRO TIP: There are both spring-blooming and fall-blooming crocus, so check plant catalogs to see what works well in your hardiness zone.

*Favorite varieties include 'Golden Yellow' and 'Cream Beauty'.

Common Name crocus

Botanical Name *Crocus vernus*

Plant Family Iridaceae

USDA Hardiness Zones 3–8

Soil Type well-drained

Soil pH neutral

Sun Exposure full or partial sun

Mature Plant Size height: up to 6 inches; width: 1 to 3 inches

Bloom Time spring

Flower Color purple, blue, yellow, orange, pink, white

Native Area South Europe, North Africa, Asia

Daffodil

To me, daffodils are the best early spring–flowering bulbs. They are deer-resistant, grow with ease, can be bought in bulk, and there are lots of options to choose from in a range of colors and petals. From single to double flowering and large-cupped varieties, daffodils make a statement when planted en masse.

PRO TIP: Choosing different daffodil varieties will help extend the bloom time overall.

*Favorite varieties include 'Apricot Whirl', 'Tender Beauty', and 'Pink Charm'.

Common Name daffodil

Botanical Name *Narcissus*

Plant Family Amaryllidaceae

USDA Hardiness Zones 3–8

Soil Type
medium to heavy, loamy

Soil pH 6.9–7.0

Sun Exposure
full sun, partial shade

Mature Plant Size
height: 8 to 18 inches;
width: 6 to 8 inches

Bloom Time spring

Flower Color
yellow, white, pink, orange

Native Area
Europe, Northern Africa

Tulip

Tulips, one of the first flowers to bloom in the spring, have blossoms that last a few weeks and look incredible even as the colorful petals begin to drop. You can find tulips in almost any color with different-shaped blooms. They make a bold statement in the early spring garden but do need protection from deer damage.

*Favorite varieties include 'Apricot Impressions', 'Palmyra', 'Foxtrot', and 'La Belle Epoque'.

Common Name tulip

Botanical Name *Tulipa*

Plant Family Liliaceae

USDA Hardiness Zones 3–8

Soil Type medium moisture, well-drained

Soil pH 6.0–7.0

Sun Exposure full sun

Mature Plant Size
height: 4 to 24 inches;
width: 6 to 9 inches

Bloom Time
mid-to-late spring

Flower Color cream, gold, orange, pink, purple

Native Area Southern Europe, Central Asia

Hyacinth

Hyacinths are beautiful early spring flowers that have an incredible aroma. Plant them near a deck, porch, or patio where you can enjoy their fragrance. They work well behind crocus but in front of tulips and daffodils.

*Favorite varieties include 'Purple Sensation' and 'Gipsy Queen'.

Common Name hyacinth

Botanical Name
Hyacinthus orientalis

Plant Family Hyacinthaceae

USDA Hardiness Zones 4–8

Soil Type well-drained, medium moisture

Soil pH acidic, alkaline, neutral

Sun Exposure full sun

Mature Plant Size
height: 8 to 12 inches;
width: 3 to 6 inches

Bloom Time spring

Flower Color
red, white, blue, purple

Native Area Eurasia, Mediterranean, Southern Turkey

Muscari (Grape Hyacinth)

Muscari is an easy-care bulb that should be planted by the dozen, as they are quite small and look so pretty when planted en masse. They are aromatic and bring a lot of texture and color to the front of gardens or rock borders.

*My favorite variety is Muscari Armeniacum.

Common Name
grape hyacinth

Botanical Name
Muscari armeniacum

Plant Family Asparagaceae

USDA Hardiness Zones 4–8

Soil Type well-drained

Soil pH acidic, neutral

Sun Exposure
full to partial sun

Mature Plant Size
height: 6 to 9 inches;
width: 2 to 6 inches

Bloom Time spring

Flower Color cobalt blue

Native Area
Southeastern Europe

Allium

Alliums are probably my favorite hardy bulb because they make a huge statement in the garden—and deer will completely leave them alone. They grow fairly tall with large globe-shaped flowers that don't need staking and look pretty even when the flowers fade. Plant them toward the back of the garden among perennials so you don't see the foliage when it dies back. Alliums look best when planted en masse, so group them together in odd numbers or space them out in a border so they flow throughout the garden.

*Favorite varieties include 'Globemaster' and 'Ambassador'.

Common Name
ornamental onion

Botanical Name *Allium*

Plant Family Amaryllidaceae

USDA Hardiness Zones 4–9

Soil Type well-drained, high in organic matter, loamy, sandy

Soil pH 5.5–6.5

Sun Exposure
full sun, partial shade

Mature Plant Size
height: 12 to 48 inches;
width: 6 to 24 inches

Bloom Time spring, summer

Flower Color gold, pink, purple, red, white

Native Area
North America, Eurasia

Spanish Bluebell

I have to admit, I'm new to growing Spanish bluebells. They were here when we moved in, and I've done nothing with them—and I love them! The flower color is striking, and they look beautiful planted in front of my azaleas.

*Favorite varieties include 'Excelsior Blue' and 'Dainty Maid Pink'.

Common Name Spanish bluebell

Botanical Name
Hyacinthoides hispanica

Plant Family Liliaceae

USDA Hardiness Zones 3–8

Soil Type well-drained

Soil pH acidic, neutral

Sun Exposure
partial sun, partial shade

Mature Plant Size
height: 6 to 18 inches;
width: 6 to 12 inches

Bloom Time spring

Flower Color lavender-blue

Native Area Spain, Portugal, Northwest Africa

SPRING-FLOWERING BULBS
THAT LOOK GOOD TOGETHER

Sun—Tulip, daffodil, and allium

Sun—Crocus, grape hyacinth, and tulip

Sun—Grape hyacinth, tulip, and daffodil

Sun with Perennials and Annuals—Allium, coneflower, nepeta, salvia, creeping phlox, myosotis, tulip, and pansy

Sun with Perennials and Annuals—Allium, baptisia, snapdragon, peony, nepeta, creeping phlox, tulip, daffodil, and pansy

Partial Shade with Perennials and Annuals—Bleeding heart, Virginia bluebell, brunnera, hellebore, Spanish bluebell, hyacinth, and crocus

Spring-flowering bulbs are a great easy-care choice for gardeners who want to add color and interest to their gardens in the early spring while other plants are still dormant. If you are just starting out as a gardener, I recommend getting a good season of growing annuals under your belt, then planting spring-flowering bulbs in the fall for a beautiful garden that will give you a succession of flowers.

CHAPTER SEVEN

Easy-Care Flowering Shrubs

———

Whether you are growing a mixed border or wanting to add foundation plantings around your home, tucking in shrubs that bloom is another easy way to grow a flower garden. Flowering shrubs have great visual impact, add interest to the landscape, and can even be grown in containers.

You can choose flowering shrubs that bloom at different times during the season, produce berries, or have gorgeous flowers that smell amazing.

But the best part? Flowering shrubs oftentimes have foliage with pretty shapes and seasonal color that add greater interest to the garden even when the flowers fade.

When it comes to flowering shrubs, you need to keep in mind the plant's maturity size because if you don't, you'll create a lot more work for yourself in the long run. So, before you plant, read the plant tags and make sure you've given your flowering shrubs enough space to grow to their eventual size.

Shrubs as Foundation Plantings

While foundation plantings add warmth and character to the entrance of a home, they can sometimes get a bit unruly if they're planted incorrectly or left untamed. It's less work to plant wisely, as you won't need to prune as often to control the plant's size or to keep it from blocking windows and doors.

Look for small-to-midsize deciduous shrubs and evergreens to add interest, and avoid plants that will grow too tall and too wide for your space. And don't guestimate—use a measuring tape to make sure you have the correct-sized foundation plantings.

Shrubs in Containers

Flowering shrubs can be grown in containers, but much like perennials, they'll need some help to successfully overwinter. For greater success, choose shrubs that are two zones hardier than your gardening zone and plant them in weather-resistant containers that will not break from freezing and thawing. While it's best to let shrubs overwinter outside, they can also be moved to an unheated garage during especially harsh weather.

When planting, use good quality potting soil with amendments and add a slow-release fertilizer in spring that is okay for that particular shrub. Read the labels and always follow directions. It's recommended to plant flowering shrubs in the ground after a few years to give them more space to grow. But you can also repot a shrub in a container that is the same or one size larger than the existing container. The plant will grow larger if you repot it in the latter, so keep that in mind if your growing space is small. When repotting, gently remove as much soil from the root ball as you can so you can replant it in fresh soil.

Pruning

We can get really in-depth here about how to properly prune flowering shrubs. But I don't want to overwhelm you—just be mindful of the overall growing size when planting, and you will not need to prune as much.

And feel free to skip down to my favorite easy-care flowering shrubs list. When you get more comfortable with growing things, come back here to learn more about pruning, because we don't just go in and cut off a bunch of branches without a little thought first.

With flowering shrubs, it's important to understand why, how, and when we need to prune, because pruning incorrectly can drastically affect flowering.

Why We Prune

- To create an aesthetically pleasing garden

- To maintain plant health

- To control growth and overall size

- To encourage fruit and flower production

- To shape a formal hedge or topiary

- To rejuvenate plants

- To keep people safe from injury

- To avoid property damage

How to Prune

As a plant matures, the top of the plant becomes more dense, which means not as much air and light can reach the interior. We prune to help open up the plant so more air and light reaches stems, main branches, and roots. This helps the plant to flower better, improves air circulation, and reduces pest and disease problems.

Before starting to prune, always clean your tools with a solution of 1:10 bleach to water ratio so you don't risk spreading disease to otherwise healthy plants. (And make sure you clean the tools again before you switch to pruning another plant.)

Also, don't just cut anywhere when you're pruning! Look for dead, diseased, or damaged branches, along with branches that cross, and prune out those first. Then cut back the suckers at the plant base, because those zap nutrients from the main plant.

There are several different types of cuts to make, and we make each one for different reasons.

Thinning

Most often, you'll make thinning cuts when pruning because it helps open up the plant while maintaining its overall aesthetic and improving its health. To thin plants, make cuts just above the parent or side branches and roughly parallel to them. Prune the entire limb or shoot, then cut off water sprouts, suckers, and smaller branches that take away energy from the main branches and add too much weight to the plant. But don't take off more than one-third of the plant's branches or you'll send it into shock.

Heading Cuts

Heading cuts are made less often, as they are intended to reduce plant height by removing part of a branch or shoot. If you planted your shrubs with their maturity size in mind, you shouldn't need to do this type of pruning very often, if at all. To make heading cuts, cut about ¼ inch above the bud or branch on a 45-degree angle that slopes down and away.

Rejuvenation

When shrubs get overgrown and look leggy, we can cut certain plants back to 4 to 10 inches from the ground when they are dormant to help rejuvenate them. You can't do this on all shrubs, but some, like weigelas, forsythias, and spireas, do well with this type of pruning. So, check the plant variety you have before doing this to make sure it will work for that particular plant.

Shearing

We make shearing cuts to manicure or shape a clean, formal hedge by removing new growth. It's more work, though, and not recommended for an easy-care garden.

When to Prune

It's super important to know when a specific plant flowers before making cuts because removing branches in different seasons can promote different things or affect flowering.

Prune spring-flowering shrubs right after they bloom, because they set buds on last year's growth. Pruning at the wrong time means you might cut off next season's blooms and dramatically decrease flowering (or have no flowers at all in the next year).

Prune summer-blooming shrubs in the late winter or early spring before the buds set or immediately after flowering.

If a landscaper maintains your shrubs, make sure they don't prune flowering shrubs at the wrong time. I've seen this happen before, so it's helpful to know what you are growing and when it needs to be pruned.

Easy-Care Flowering Shrubs You Should Grow

Here are some flowering shrubs that are easy to grow with minimal care. They have different seasonal bloom times, so if you plan it right, you can get a succession of flowers from spring through fall just from your shrubs.

Forsythia

No other shrub tells us spring has arrived quite like forsythia. It blooms early, is incredibly easy to grow, and you can even cut and force forsythia branches to bloom indoors so you can enjoy them before spring's arrival. But give forsythia room to grow in your garden, because it can easily take over an area and you'll need to keep it in check. Depending on the variety, forsythia plants are better kept in open spaces rather than around a foundation.

*Favorite varieties include Proven Winners 'Show Off' and Proven Winners 'Show Off Sugar Baby'.

Common Name forsythia

Botanical Name *Forsythia spp.*

Plant Family Oleaceae

USDA Hardiness Zones 3b–8

Soil Type sandy, loamy, clay, adaptable, moist, well-drained

Soil pH 5–8

Sun Exposure full sun

Mature Plant Size height: 2 to 10 feet; width: 2 to12 feet

Bloom Time early spring

Flower Color yellow

Native Area China and Korea

Lilac

Although lilacs bloom for a short period of time, you can't beat their spring flowers and heavenly scent. Lilacs can be a little fussy, so choose strong-willed varieties like Proven Winners 'Bloomerang' that are more disease-resistant and will provide you with a second set of flowers. Lilacs make wonderful cut flowers to bring indoors too.

*Favorite varieties include Proven Winners 'Bloomerang Purple', Proven Winners 'Baby Kim', and 'President Lincoln'.

Common Name lilac

Botanical Name
Syringa vulgaris

Plant Family Oleaceae

USDA Hardiness Zones
3–7a

Soil Type well-drained, moist

Soil pH alkaline, neutral

Sun Exposure
full sun, partial shade

Mature Plant Size
height: 8 to 16 feet;
width: 6 to 12 feet

Bloom Time spring

Flower Color blue, cream, tan, pink, purple, lavender, white

Native Area Balkan Peninsula

Rhododendron

If you have a shadier garden, rhododendrons can make a huge impact in the spring. This slow-growing evergreen shrub looks beautiful year-round and has gorgeous blooms, plus the foliage makes great filler for arrangements. Rhododendrons love acidic soil, so make sure your soil has what it takes to grow them. They make a great foundation planting but look amazing in mixed borders too. Rhododendrons are not deer-resistant and do require protection from wildlife.

*Favorite varieties include 'Jane Grant' and Proven Winners 'Dandy Man Pink'.

Common Name
rhododendron

Botanical Name
Rhododendron

Plant Family Ericaceae

USDA Hardiness Zones 4–8

Soil Type well-drained, moist, high in organic matter

Soil pH acidic

Sun Exposure
dappled sunlight, deep shade, partial shade

Mature Plant Size
height: 6 to 10 feet;
width: 5 to 8 feet

Bloom Time spring

Flower Color gold, orange, pink, purple, red, white

Native Area much of the United States, Europe, Asia, and northeastern Australia

Azalea

Azaleas are another shade-loving evergreen flowering shrub that prefers acidic soil, so check before planting to make sure you have the right growing conditions for them. Azaleas make great foundation plantings but look amazing in mixed borders too. They are not deer-resistant and need protection from wildlife.

*Favorite varieties include 'Marie Hoffman' and Proven Winners 'Perfecto Mundo Double Pink'.

Common Name azalea

Botanical Name
Rhododendron prinophyllum

Plant Family Ericaceae

USDA Hardiness Zones
6b–8a, varies by species

Soil Type
well-drained, organic

Soil pH acidic

Sun Exposure shade

Mature Plant Size
height: 3 to 20 feet;
width: 3 to 20 feet

Bloom Time
early spring, midsummer

Flower Color white, pink, red, purple; some have different patterns

Native Area Asia, Europe, North America

Spirea

Spireas come in lots of different varieties and are very easy to grow. These low-growing, deer-resistant shrubs can be planted along a foundation or within a mixed border. While the flowers are pretty, the different colors of spirea foliage bring their A game in the fall when the leaves change.

*Favorite varieties include Proven Winners 'Double Play Candy Corn' and Proven Winners 'Double Play Red'.

Common Name spirea

Botanical Name *Spiraea spp.*

Plant Family Rosaceae

USDA Hardiness Zones 3–9, depending on variety

Soil Type well-drained, moist, shallow, rocky

Soil pH acidic, neutral

Sun Exposure full sun; tolerant to partial shade, but it's not preferred

Mature Plant Size height: 36 to 60 inches; width: 36 to 60 inches

Bloom Time spring

Flower Color white, pink, purple

Native Area Central and Eastern Asia

Weigela

If you want an easy-care flowering shrub that blooms in the spring, attracts hummingbirds, and has attractive foliage, plant a weigela. This small-to-mid-size shrub has the prettiest flowers and looks amazing along a foundation or within a mixed border.

*Favorite varieties include Proven Winners 'Wine & Roses' and 'Dark Horse'.

Common Name weigela

Botanical Name *Weigela florida*

Plant Family Caprifoliaceae

USDA Hardiness Zones 4–8

Soil Type well-drained, moist

Soil pH acidic, alkaline, neutral

Sun Exposure dappled sunlight, full sun, partial shade

Mature Plant Size height: 2 to 10 feet; width: 2 to 12 feet

Bloom Time spring, summer

Flower Color pink, red, white

Native Area Northern China, Korea, Japan

Ninebark

I'd always wanted to grow ninebark but lacked the space in my former garden. But I have a few ninebark shrubs in my current garden, and let me tell you—they are fabulous! From the dark-colored foliage to the pretty pink flowers that bloom in the spring, it's a beautiful shrub that adds lots of color throughout the growing season with little to no work from you. Give these shrubs the space they need to grow and you'll be rewarded with a plant that has a graceful arching habit and a strong visual interest that also adds some height to a garden.

*Favorite varieties include Proven Winners 'Summer Wine Black' and Proven Winners 'Tiny Wine'.

Common Name ninebark

Botanical Name
Physocarpus Opulifolius

Plant Family Rosaceae

USDA Hardiness Zones 2–7

Soil Type well-drained, tolerates a wide range of soil conditions

Soil pH 5.0–8.0; acidic to alkaline

Sun Exposure full sun, tolerates partial shade

Mature Plant Size
height: 3 to 8 feet; width: 4 to 8 feet

Bloom Time
May to early June

Flower Color white to pinkish

Native Area Central and Eastern North America

Elderberry

Elderberry is another one of those shrubs that I'd always wanted to grow but lacked the garden space to plant until we moved. We now have an elderberry bush in the backyard garden, and it is as beautiful as I thought it would be! You can't beat the lacy, almost-black foliage, and it produces pretty pink flower heads in the spring that smell unbelievable.

*Favorite varieties include Proven Winners 'Black Lace' and Proven Winners 'Black Beauty'.

Common Name elderberry

Botanical Name *Sambucus canadensis*

Plant Family Adoxaceae

USDA Hardiness Zones 4–8

Soil Type prefers rich, moist soil; can tolerate both wet and dry soil

Soil pH slightly acidic

Sun Exposure sun, partial shade

Mature Plant Size height: 5 to 12 feet; width: 6 to 12 feet

Bloom Time spring and summer, fruits in fall

Flower Color summer: small white flowers; late summer to fall: purple-black drupe

Native Area North America, Venezuela, and Brazil

Callicarpa Americana (only)

Check with your local cooperative extension before planting callicarpa, also called American beautyberry, to make sure it's not on the invasive plant species list where you garden. I love to grow it, not so much for the flowers but because it produces these *gorgeous* purple berries in the fall. While the flowers are insignificant, those berries and fall foliage are why you want to grow beautyberries. Callicarpa americana is a midsized flowering shrub with a graceful arching habit, so make sure you give it ample growing room before planting it.

*Favorite varieties include 'Early Amethyst' and Proven Winners 'Pearl Glam'.

Common Name
American beautyberry

Botanical Name
Callicarpa americana

Plant Family Lamiaceae

USDA Hardiness Zones
6–10

Soil Type sandy, loamy, clay

Soil pH acidic, slightly alkaline

Sun Exposure partial sun, partial shade

Mature Plant Size
height: 3 to 8 feet;
width: 4 to 8 feet

Bloom Time spring

Flower Color lavender

Native Area Florida

Rose of Sharon

Rose of Sharon is another easy-care shrub that is almost no-fail. The flowers are beautiful in the summer, and these plants look great in the back of mixed borders. Give them room to grow, then just let these deer-resistant plants do the rest.

*Favorite varieties include Proven Winners 'White Chiffon' and Proven Winners 'Azurri Blue Satin'.

Common Name
rose of Sharon

Botanical Name
Hibiscus syriacus

Plant Family Malvaceae

USDA Hardiness Zones
5B–9A

Soil Type clay, loamy, sandy, well-drained, occasionally wet

Soil pH acidic

Sun Exposure partial shade, partial sun, full sun

Mature Plant Size
height: 8 to 12 feet;
width: 4 to 10 feet

Bloom Time summer

Flower Color blue, lavender, pink, purple, red, white

Native Area Asia, in a range from China to India

Caryopteris

Caryopteris is a low-mounding shrub that produces the prettiest blue flowers, which pollinators love. It is easy to grow and deer-resistant, and you should plant one if you have the space for it.

*Favorite varieties include 'Longwood Blue' and Proven Winners Beyond Midnight'.

Common Name
bluebeard, blue mist shrub

Botanical Name
Caryopteris × clandonensis

Plant Family Lamiaceae

USDA Hardiness Zones 6–9

Soil Type
loose, well-drained, loamy

Soil pH 6.5–7.5

Sun Exposure full sun

Mature Plant Size
height: 24 to 36 inches;
width: 24 to 36 inches

Bloom Time
late summer, early fall

Flower Color blue

Native Area East Asia

Viburnum

Viburnums are generally deer-resistant and can make great foundation plantings (depending on their size) while adding seasonal color and interest with their aromatic flowers, foliage, and berries. Birds love the berries, so adding these plants to your garden is a great way to feed the birds in your area during colder months. Make sure you give viburnums room to grow because they can be a sizable shrub.

*Favorite varieties include Proven Winners 'Spice Girl', Proven Winners 'Spice Baby', and Proven Winners 'Blue Muffin'.

Common Name viburnum

Botanical Name
Viburnum spp.

Plant Family Adoxaceae

USDA Hardiness Zones 2–9

Soil Type moist, well-drained

Soil pH neutral, acidic

Sun Exposure
full sun, partial shade

Maturity Height and Width
height: 3 to 20 feet;
width: 3 to 12 feet

Bloom Time spring, summer

Flower Color
cream, white, pink

Native Area North America

FLOWERING SHRUBS THAT LOOK GOOD TOGETHER

Part Sun—Ninebark, hydrangea, and viburnum

Part Sun—Abelia, weigela, and spirea

Full Sun—Limelight hydrangea, purple smoketree, and callicarpa

Full Sun—Ninebark, limelight hydrangea, and caryopteris

Shade—Rhododendron, azalea, and andromeda

Shade—Rhododendron, bottlebrush buckeye, and mountain laurel

Flowering shrubs are a great way to add large-scale color, texture, and interest to the garden with minimal care. They can provide year-round interest, as many have striking evergreen or fall foliage color, winter bark, or attractive seed heads, in addition to flowers and berries (if any). You probably already have some flowering shrubs growing in your garden. If you do, take more of an interest in them and learn more about them. Watch how they grow and notice how they look throughout the seasons. As you gain experience gardening, consider tucking more flowering shrubs into your landscape.

CHAPTER EIGHT

Grow and Enjoy Hydrangeas

———

Because hydrangeas are my favorite flowers and are so popular with my readers, they deserve their own chapter. Many homeowners grow them whether they garden or not, and I'm often asked about hydrangeas and their care.

There are lots of different types of hydrangeas to grow. You can find reblooming varieties while others will bloom once and be done until the following season. It's helpful to know what varieties of hydrangeas you have, because that drives how you can best care for them.

And while hydrangeas look gorgeous in the landscape, the flowers are equally as beautiful inside the home. Whether used in fresh or dried arrangements, hydrangeas are a great way to bring the outdoors in.

Planting and Growing Hydrangeas

Depending on the variety, hydrangeas generally prefer morning sun and afternoon shade. But there are some varieties that can handle more sunlight, so read the plant tag to see what kind of light conditions your hydrangea needs. When planting or relocating hydrangeas, it's best to do so in the early spring or fall, replanting them in soil rich in organic matter.

Pay close attention to drainage because hydrangeas do not like wet feet. You'll know your hydrangea is getting too much water if its leaves develop brown edges or drop off. Alternatively, if hydrangeas receive too little water, they will let you know through droopy foliage that revives after watering.

If you are growing hydrangeas in containers, amend the potting soil and feed them with organic fertilizer in the spring. To overwinter with greater success, choose a hydrangea that is two times hardier than your zone. It is best to let them overwinter outdoors, but where winters are cold you can also move them inside an unheated garage or shed for protection. It's recommended to plant potted hydrangeas in the ground after a year or two, or repot in a new container that is one size larger, to give the roots room to grow.

Favorite Hydrangeas

*Favorite varieties include 'Endless Summer', Proven Winners 'Limelight Prime', and Proven Winners 'Little Quick Fire'.

Common Name hydrangea

Botanical Name *Hydrangea spp.*

Plant Family Hydrangeaceae

USDA Hardiness Zones 3–9

Soil Type well-drained

Soil pH different pH creates different flower colors (see page 153)

Sun Exposure sun, partial sun

Mature Plant Size height: up to 15 feet depending on variety; width: 4 to 6 feet

Bloom Time fall, spring, summer

Flower Color white, pink, blue, purple

Native Area China, Korea, Japan

Common Pest and Disease Problems

When planted in the right place, hydrangeas are easy-care and low-maintenance. However, there are some things to look out for.

Powdery mildew and blackspot are common issues when hydrangeas are planted in heavy shade, receive a lot of water, and have poor soil drainage. To remedy powdery mildew and blackspot, clean them up by getting rid of the diseased leaves, and relocate your hydrangeas in their dormant season (early spring or late fall) to a sunnier spot with better drainage.

When hydrangeas receive too much sun and are watered from above, you might see some rust spots. To correct this, always water them in the mornings at the base of plants. And if you suspect your hydrangea is getting too much sun, relocate it to a slightly shadier spot in the spring or fall.

Slugs and snails can be a problem for hydrangeas, but you can deter them by using snail bait. Hydrangeas are also susceptible to deer damage and need protection from wildlife.

Fertilizing Hydrangeas

In general, hydrangeas do not need to be fertilized. Instead, amend the soil with high-quality organic matter. Overfertilizing can burn tender plant roots.

When hydrangeas are fed too much nitrogen, the foliage will look really lush and beautiful, but you'll get fewer flowers. This is important to know because grass fertilizer is high in nitrogen, which greens up lawns. If grass fertilizer is fed too close to hydrangea plants, your hydrangeas will not flower as much, if at all.

If you see your hydrangea not doing well or not blooming for any reason, resist the urge to use fertilizer on it. It likely does not need it, and you'll do more harm than good.

How to Change a Hydrangea Plant's Flower Color

Hydrangeas are sensitive to soil pH, which can affect the color of the flowers. With the exception of white-flowering varieties, acidic soil conditions cause flowers to be more blue or purple. In such cases, soil pH is typically less than 7. Alternatively, more neutral soils produce flowers that are pink or red.

To increase acidity, amend the soil with sulfates like coffee grounds. To increase the alkaline in your soil, add garden lime.

I don't recommend messing with a hydrangea's flower color. Let the plant do what it wants without any interference from you. It's better for the plant and easier for you. But if you choose to attempt to change the color, only do it with plants that are well-established, and keep an eye on overall plant health.

Pruning Hydrangeas

It is important to know what type of hydrangea you have so you know when to prune it. Too often, home gardeners and landscapers blindly cut hydrangeas back during their fall garden cleanup and mistakenly cut off next year's flowers without even realizing it. Therefore, it's super important to know what you are growing so you don't accidentally cut off future blooms.

There are three different hydrangea categories that have different pruning needs, depending on whether the plant flowers on old or new growth.

- *Hydrangea macrophylla* blooms on old wood.

- *Hydrangea arborescens* and *Hydrangea paniculata* bloom on new growth.

- The *macrophylla* cultivar *'Endless Summer'* is everblooming, and blooms on both old and new wood.

Everblooming and other *macrophylla* hydrangeas that bloom on old wood (last year's growth) should be pruned when the flowers start to fade. If you cut them back between fall and early spring, they won't flower because the buds will have been trimmed off.

Hydrangeas that bloom on new growth should be cut back in late winter or early spring. For example, I cut my *Hydrangea paniculata* back hard the first seasonable day in late winter or early spring, and it blooms beautifully every fall. Thus, timing is critical.

Some hydrangeas, like climbing and oakleaf, need little to no pruning at all if you plant them in the right spot given their size at maturity. I had an oakleaf hydrangea for at least 15 years that I never touched and it bloomed beautifully every year.

Not sure what variety you have? Reach out to your local cooperative extension or master gardener program and ask them to help identify the plant for you.

How to Prune a Hydrangea

When pruning hydrangeas, cut on a 45-degree angle about ½ to 1 inch above a budding node.

If your hydrangea is well-established, it will have totally woody branches that die back yearly inside the shrub. Cut these branches down to the ground to promote new growth at the base of the plant. But I strongly recommend waiting until the whole plant is lush and green before doing this. It might not look great, but you won't risk sacrificing any flowers.

Why Your Hydrangea Isn't Blooming

There are a few reasons why hydrangeas fail to bloom or why they produce fewer flowers. If this is happening with your plant, ask yourself these questions and we'll deep dive into these issues in the next few pages.

- Did the hydrangea come from a florist or was it gifted to you?

- Is it planted in the right location for its variety?

- Did you prune it at the right time?

- Did you test the soil?

- Did it receive too much fertilizer?

- How long ago was it planted?

- Did you have severe weather or a late frost that could have damaged the buds?

Why Gift or Florist Hydrangeas May Not Bloom Again

If a hydrangea was received as a gift, packaged with pretty foil or plastic wrap, the hydrangea is likely a florist or gift hydrangea. These hydrangeas are greenhouse-raised to profusely bloom at the point of sale and oftentimes don't do as well once they are planted in the garden. If you receive one as a gift and decide to plant it in the garden, know that it may or may not flower and keep your expectations low.

Planting Location Matters

Check the hardiness zone for the variety of hydrangea you have and make sure it's zoned for your climate. It's possible for plant roots to survive a cold winter, but the flower buds may succumb if they bloom on old growth. These plants might need to be protected by wrapping them in burlap to insulate the buds.

If the hydrangea is getting too much shade, it will not bloom. Generally, hydrangeas prefer morning sun with afternoon shade and need at least four to six hours of dappled sunlight per day. Check light conditions and transplant the hydrangea to a sunnier spot in your yard if the current location is too shady.

Pruning at the Right Time Matters

Most often, hydrangeas lack blooms because they were pruned at the wrong time. Know what type of hydrangea you have so you know when to prune it.

Soil Quality Matters

If your hydrangea has few flowers or fails to bloom at all, test the soil. A soil test may reveal nutritional deficiencies or let you know that there's too much nitrogen in the soil, which promotes foliage instead of blooms. If high levels of nitrogen are present, consider how much and how often fertilizer is applied, then reevaluate how the area should be fertilized, if at all, in the future.

Overfertilizing

Stop fertilizing the hydrangea and see if that improves flowering the following season. Instead of adding fertilizer, work on improving the overall soil quality.

Recently Planted Hydrangeas

Hydrangeas may not flower within the first few years of planting because they are focusing on developing good, healthy root systems. I planted a climbing hydrangea that took several years to bloom. Be patient and give them time to establish their root systems before expecting any flowers. As long as the plant is green and otherwise looks healthy, it may just need more time.

Weather

Severe weather can damage hydrangea buds that are set on old wood, which can hinder flowering. They may need additional protection in places with severe winters.

How to Get More Hydrangeas for Free

If you want to expand your garden with more hydrangeas but want to keep it budget-friendly, hydrangeas are very easy to propagate. We won't go too in-depth here, so go to my blog to find more information if you want to try this [1], but here are three ways hydrangeas can be propagated:

- Root cuttings (this is done by cutting a branch that did not flower, dipping it in some rooting hormone, then planting it in vermiculite or sterile soil)

- Layering (this is done by taking a branch, weighing it down with a rock, then burying it under soil until it takes root)

- Dividing (see page 87 in chapter 5)

More Ways to Enjoy Hydrangeas

While hydrangeas are fun to grow in the landscape, the flowers are even more enjoyable to cut for indoor use. Here are a few tips and tricks for enjoying the beautiful blooms in your home.

How to Cut Hydrangea Flowers for Arrangements

If you are cutting hydrangea flowers from your garden, there are a few things to keep in mind to help the flowers retain as much moisture as possible.

- Always cut hydrangeas in the mornings when the weather is cool.

- Look for blooms that are completely open before cutting.

- Always use a clean set of pruners.

---

1   https://stacyling.com/how-to-propagate-hydrangeas-in-7-easy-steps/

❋ Cut stems on an angle, remove all the leaves, and immediately drop the cut flowers into a container of fresh water.

How to Keep Freshly Cut Hydrangea Flowers from Wilting in an Arrangement

Have you ever cut or bought fresh hydrangea flowers from the market and put them in a vase with water, only to see them droop within a day?

It's sad when this happens, but the good news is, we can prevent the wilt and even fix it after it occurs. Freshly cut hydrangeas droop because they self-heal from the initial cut. The cut stem forms a substance over the wound to heal itself, so the water has trouble reaching the blooms. And when the flowers don't get enough water, they wilt. Luckily, there are a few easy fixes for this problem. With proper care, hydrangea flowers can last a long time in an arrangement.

Hot Water Method

❋ Boil water.

❋ Have a vase of room-temperature water ready to hold the arrangement.

❋ Cut the hydrangea stems again on an angle to the desired length of the arrangement. (Some people like to smash the bottoms of the stems so they take in more water. I've never done this, but I've heard it works.)

❋ Stand the hydrangea stems in hot water for 30 seconds.

❋ Immediately drop the cut flowers into room-temperature water.

❋ Arrange the flowers to your liking.

Alum Spice Method

Alum is a spice used for pickling and canning. But did you know that it can also be used to help keep hydrangeas from wilting?

- Put some alum spice in a narrow container to dip the hydrangea stems in.

- Have a vase with room-temperature water ready.

- Recut the hydrangea stems on an angle to the desired length of the arrangement.

- Dip the bottom ½ inch of the stem into the alum.

- Drop the cut flowers into the vase with water.

- Arrange the flowers to your liking.

How to Revive Wilted Blooms

If you made an arrangement with freshly cut hydrangeas and the flowers start to wilt, there's an easy way to revive them so they will perk up and look pretty again.

- If the arrangement's water is more than a day old, dump it out and replace it with fresh water.

- Soak the blooms for several hours. (I like to do this in the kitchen sink.)

- Recut all the stems at an angle.

Choose and follow either the hot water method or the alum spice method to finish reviving the blooms. If the arrangement is already a few days old, blooms may be more difficult to revive. But you can always give it a shot!

How to Dry Hydrangea Flowers

Dried hydrangea flowers make beautiful seasonal decor inside your home. I love how they look, whether they are tucked into a basket or displayed in a vase. And they can last a very long time too.

It's ridiculously easy to dry hydrangeas. Here's how to do it.

- Allow the blooms to dry naturally on the plant, which is typically about 6 to 8 weeks after they start flowering (August through October-ish). They are ready to cut when the petals look a little more vintage than bright and the flowers feel a little papery. If you cut them when the flowers are fresh, they won't dry well.

- Find blooms on the plant that meet this criteria and cut the stems about 12 to 18 inches long, varying the lengths because it will help with the drying process when they are grouped together.

- Remove all leaves from the stems and drop the cut hydrangeas into a bucket of water.

- Grab a few glass jars or vases and fill each with about 2 to 3 inches of water.

- Drop the cut hydrangeas into the water, but avoid overcrowding the blooms in the jars so that they get enough air circulation.

- Allow the water to evaporate naturally and don't add any more water.

- As the water evaporates, the hydrangea flowers will naturally start drying.

How to Make a Simple Hydrangea Wreath

Making a wreath from hydrangea flowers is so fun to do, and it makes beautiful fall decor. This is also a great way to repurpose those old wreaths you have lying around.

SUPPLIES
- pruners
- container to collect the blooms
- grapevine wreath or another wreath form

DIRECTIONS
1. Buy or use an old grapevine wreath you have lying around.
2. Using sharp pruners, cut vintage-looking, papery hydrangea flowers about 8 to 10 inches long.
3. Collect blooms in a basket or other container. If you are not making the wreath right away, drop the cut hydrangea flowers immediately in water and keep them there until you are ready.
4. Remove all the leaves from the stems.
5. Cut the stems down to about 4 to 6 inches so they are long enough to securely stick into the grapevine wreath but short enough to not stick out of the wreath.
6. Add hydrangea flowers, working from left to right, until you fill the wreath. If you prefer the wreath half full, that's fine too.
7. Hang your hydrangea wreath when it's finished, but keep it out of direct sunlight for best results. The flowers will dry right on the wreath!

If you've made it this far in the book, I probably don't need to sell you on all the reasons why you should grow hydrangeas. In fact, you might already have them in your landscape. But if you don't? Run to the nursery and pick up one hydrangea plant that is suited for the conditions you have in your garden. The flowers are gorgeous in the landscape, the colors are amazing, the plants are easy to grow, and the blooms can be enjoyed inside your home too. Plant hydrangeas in a container or in your landscape and enjoy them for years to come!

CHAPTER NINE

Container Gardening

If you have little growing space, want to start small, or are looking to add flowers to hardscaped areas, container gardening is a great option. It affords the opportunity to garden regardless of the size, shape, or location of your garden and outdoor living spaces.

And if you are just starting out gardening or are looking to achieve a small success, I highly recommend starting with one container in a location that's easy for you to care for so you can learn how to grow things. There are so many things you can grow in a container, and it's a great opportunity to learn gardening basics in a very manageable way.

Container gardens are fun to design and are one of my favorite ways to garden because you can play with different flowers, textures, and dimensions in pots that can be moved around.

Whether you keep your container gardens simple or create something more elaborate with different plants, they are the perfect addition both indoors and out to create a cozy, welcoming home.

Choosing Your Container

Before purchasing plants, think about what style, color, and size containers you want to use. I recommend working with oversized or larger planters because they do not dry out as quickly, which means less work for you in terms of watering. Not to mention, they can hold more plants and flowers, thus creating greater visual impact.

Choosing the right container is important for both how you like to garden and your overall decorating style. Do you prefer farmhouse to French Country style? Does color or material matter? You'll want to choose containers that fit the look you love while also considering your price point, because some containers can get expensive!

Types of Gardening Containers

In container gardening, it's not just the aesthetic that matters, because the type of material your containers are made from can affect how you garden. For example, some planters are more porous, so they'll draw out moisture, causing the soil to dry out quicker. Other containers can't be left outdoors all winter long because they are subject to cracking in freezing and thawing conditions. This means what you grow and how you care for plants in containers will be affected by the type of container you use.

Whatever you choose, make sure that each container has good drainage holes, as not all containers have them. If you need to add some, grab a drill and make a few holes in the bottom of the container so water can drain out and the plants won't get waterlogged.

If you are reusing planters, clean and disinfect them with a 1:10 bleach to water ratio and some soap before adding new plants and soil to them.

Plastic

In general, plastic or resin-type containers are weather-resistant, durable, and light enough to move around. Some are so well-made, they almost look like true terra-cotta, stone, or concrete. But they are not porous, so the soil will retain more moisture. As such, it's much easier to overwater plants in these types of containers. So, keep an eye on the soil and note how much water they retain.

These types of containers can be very budget-friendly, depending on the style. But some plastic containers or resin pots don't look all that amazing. If the aesthetic doesn't matter, then use whatever you want. But if you want a container to look really beautiful and authentic? Then you've got to be choosy and really look at the details. Ask yourself, *Does this look like the real thing?* If it doesn't, put it back on the shelf.

Wood

Wooden containers come in various sizes and shapes and are generally made from pine, teak, or cedar. When planting in wooden containers, add some sort of lining to the inside of the pot, because over time that wood will break down and rot. If you don't care about future wood rot, then lining wood pots may not be an issue for you. Cedar and teak last longer than some other types of wood, but regardless, I'd still add a liner that's BPA-free to extend the life of a wooden container.

Metal

Metal containers add interesting texture and color to the garden. They are durable, last a long time, and weather well when exposed to the elements. But they are not porous, so be careful when watering and watch to make sure they don't retain too much moisture.

Terra-cotta

Terra-cotta pots, which are made from clay, come in lots of beautiful shapes and a variety of sizes that are readily available. Clay pots draw moisture away from plants, which dries the soil out more quickly. Thus, terra-cotta planters can help plants that tend to get overwatered. On the other hand, you might need to water plants in these containers more often, so keep your eye on the soil. Terra-cotta pots are perfect for succulent-type plants that prefer drier soil conditions.

Since they are made from clay, terra-cotta pots break more easily and are not made to withstand extreme winter conditions. Handle them with care, and bring them indoors when winter arrives.

Also, clay pots can get pretty heavy if they are on the larger size and filled with soil. When working with larger containers, you may need a dolly to help move them around.

Concrete

Concrete pots are also durable, readily available, and can last for several years. If you live in an area where freezing temperatures occur, you will need to insulate them well to prevent the pots from cracking during cold weather, and you will need to move them indoors if possible.

I had not used concrete planters until recently, when we found some *gorgeous* ones tucked away in the garden shed shortly after moving here. But after having used them, I love them. However, they are extremely heavy, so be mindful where you place them because they will not be easy to move around later.

Self-Watering

There are also self-watering containers available that have reservoirs at the bottom that help make watering easier for gardeners. Self-watering containers reduce the amount of time spent watering and are helpful to use in spaces that are not in close proximity to a water source.

Think Outside the Box

There are lots of items out there that can be repurposed as garden planters, so don't limit yourself to just the above options. I *love* to shop at thrift stores, flea markets, and antique malls for different containers that could potentially hold plants. You can find the coolest items that can be flipped into a unique planter for next to nothing.

Choosing Plants

When designing a planter with more than one plant in mind, consider the container design technique: thriller, filler, and spiller. I use this design method with almost all my container garden and centerpiece ideas when I am using more than one type of plant.

- *Thriller* plants add height and drama.

- *Filler* plants create fullness and fill in the gaps.

- *Spiller* plants trail over the edges and spill over to soften the hard lines.

The neat thing about using the thriller, filler, and spiller method is that some plants can fall into more than one category. As you work with more and more plants and flowers, you'll learn how they grow during a season so you can design a container with more intention.

Here are some examples of plants that I enjoy working with and buy almost yearly, depending on what the nursery has in stock. As always, check the plant labels so you can group plants with similar light and watering conditions.

- **Thrillers:** Cordyline, fountain grass (or other grassy-looking plant), canna lily, millet, caladium, colocasia, and coleus

- **Fillers:** Geranium, begonia, impatiens, marigold, pansy, coleus, petunia, alyssum, and baby's-breath euphorbia

- **Spillers:** Petunia, angelonia, calibrachoa, bacopa, sweet potato vine, licorice plant, scaevola, nasturium, ivy, and lantana

When shopping for plants at the nursery, I like to see how they pair together. Even if I don't have my container with me, I play around with those plants right on the cart, arranging them in ways I think I'd use in my planters. It's not always precise, but it's pretty close when I go to plant them.

While I'm standing there in the nursery, I ask myself, *Does this look aesthetically pleasing?* I take into consideration the foliage, blooms, plant size, and the overall growing habit of each plant.

But you also need to keep in mind where your outdoor planters will be located and what each plant's watering requirements are when selecting plants. Shade versus sun matters, and you don't want to mix in the same pot plants that prefer moist soil with plants that prefer drier conditions. So, make sure you read those plant tags!

Plant an odd number of plants in each container so the overall arrangement is more pleasing to the eye. But make sure you purchase enough plants to fit in the container you are using. Since growing seasons tend to be short, I recommend stuffing containers full until you can't fit in any more plants. This not only helps prevent weeds from popping up, but it also makes the planter look more lush and full from the outset.

As an aside, I almost rarely have to weed my planters, so if you want less weeding in your flower gardening life, create some beautiful container gardens!

Planting in Containers

If you do not already have potting soil in your containers, fill them with fresh, organic potting soil. And if your containers already have soil in them, remove some of the old soil and add fresh potting soil mix with soil amendments

already mixed in. Your container plants need to grow in fresh soil that is rich in organic matter or they won't thrive.

Every time we water our planters, soil nutrients wash out, so always add fresh soil to your containers when planting new plants in them. I tend to remove about half of the old soil, then add new soil underneath and around new plants so the roots have healthy new soil to grow in.

Potting Tips

Before adding potting soil, place a layer of weed fabric into the bottom of the container. Weed fabric allows water to seep out the drainage holes while keeping the soil inside.

To keep large planters lightweight and more budget-friendly, fill the bottom one-fourth of a container with crushed plastic nursery pots, then fill the pot with soil and plants. This is a great way to reuse old pots from the nursery, your containers will be significantly lighter to move around, and it will save you money on soil.

If you are using tall, thin containers, consider weighting them down with some rocks at the bottom so they don't blow over in the wind.

When planting a container using the thriller, filler, and spiller technique, I usually start with the thriller plant in the center, then work my way out and around with filler plants, and finally add with spiller plants at the edges. If the planter will be maintained against a wall, I'll plant the thriller toward the back, then add the filler and spiller out, around, and down.

While working on your container gardens, step back a few times to see that the overall arrangement has symmetry, balance, and fullness. Since I like to stuff containers full, there is usually no room left in a pot after I finish putting in the plants. But if you want to add other elements to your containers like bows, raffia, wicker, or birdhouses, leave some space for them.

How to Plant a Container Garden

SUPPLIES
- plants
- container
- potting soil
- weed fabric
- gardening gloves
- scissors
- fertilizer
- hand trowel

DIRECTIONS

1. Gather your supplies and put on the gloves.

2. Cut the weed fabric to a size that will fit inside the container. It's less likely to shift when you add soil if you cut enough fabric to run up the sides of the container.

3. Add potting soil with a hand trowel, filling about one-half to two-thirds of the container so that plants have some soil to sit in with room for their roots to grow.

4. Check the planting depth by adding your plants while they are still in their plastic nursery pots. Match the soil line to about an inch down from the top of the container. If more soil is needed to get the right depth, add more.

5. Remove the plants from their plastic pots and fan out the roots of each plant before setting them in the bigger container. Fanning the roots encourages the plant to grow out into the potting soil.

6. Backfill with potting soil, tamping it down as you go to remove the air pockets.

7. Add a slow-release fertilizer and water well.

Watering and Fertilizing

Container gardens need to be watered and fertilized on a regular basis to keep the plants healthy, blooming, and looking good. Since nutrients flush out of the soil every time you water, planters need to be fertilized.

In spring, the climate in New Jersey usually does most of the watering work for me. But in general, I recommend watering about one to two times a week when temperatures are mild. However, once the hot, humid summer temperatures hit, I water them once a day and sometimes twice a day if it's crazy hot and the containers are small. If you are using self-watering planters, how often you water will depend on the reservoir, so follow the manufacturer's recommendations.

The best rule of thumb for keeping container gardens well-watered is to keep an eye on any potted plants you have and learn how well they drain. If the plants start looking sad and droopy, it's time to water. Easy-care plants tend to be more resilient, which is why I recommend starting out with some of those listed on page 70 before advancing to more challenging flowers that might not bounce back as easily.

If you are new to gardening or think you kill things, I recommend building your confidence by putting together a simple planter or two that features just one type of flower. Spend your time and energy making this container flourish, and you can always add more plants and containers after you achieve some success with your beginner project.

Knowing When to Water Container Plantings

Watering on the same day(s) each week can be harmful to your plants because they may not always need weekly watering. Here's why.

Soil is very similar to a sponge. If you soak a sponge and hold it upright, water collects at the bottom while the top dries out. Thus, the soil surface may look and feel dry, but it may not be dry where the roots are located down below.

So, if you water on the same day every week, the soil surface might look dry, but the soil may be completely saturated where the roots are. To check, you can use a moisture meter or do the cake batter test:

- Insert your finger, a plastic knife, a popsicle stick, or something similar about an inch into the soil.

- If the tester comes out clean, it's time to water.

- If the tester comes out with some wet soil, do not water the plant yet.

- Recheck using the same process in another day or two if the tester comes out with some wet soil. If the soil is now dry, it's time to water.

Raised Garden Beds

Raised garden beds are a great way to elevate your garden from the ground. It's a wonderful option for those with bad backs or who lack mobility. And if critters are a problem in your area, it's easier to keep them out of a raised bed.

Raised garden beds are also a simple solution to poor soil quality because you can add amazing soil and amendments with ease. I have a few corrugated metal raised garden beds that work well for our vegetable garden. It's difficult for rodents to climb up the sides, and I like being able to garden without crouching down near the ground.

When setting up raised beds, it is really important to place them near a water source. Because trust me when I tell you, in the heat of summer, it will be a huge chore if they're not. It's a big pain to drag a 50-to-100-foot hose across the yard and then put it back when you're done. Been there, done that—and I won't do it again.

If you choose to DIY your own raised garden beds and plan to grow anything edible, use cedar or another type of wood that does not contain arsenic. Consider lining the insides of each bed with BPA–free plastic to keep wet soil from rotting the wood. And as an extra precaution, add chicken wire to the base to keep critters from getting into the beds from underneath.

CHAPTER TEN

Cut Flower Gardening

Through most of my gardening life, I hesitated to cut my garden flowers to enjoy indoors because I love watching them grow in the landscape. To change that mindset, I started growing flowers with the specific intent of cutting them.

And it's been awesome!

I love cutting flowers to make floral arrangements for my home, and you will too.

Just keep in mind that not all flowers grown for cutting are easy to grow. Some require more maintenance than others, so I'm going to share some easier plants for you to try if you want to get your feet wet.

How to Start a Cut Flower Garden

While you can find flowers for cutting at the nursery, the options are limited. The best way to grow a cutting garden is to start it from seed. This takes a little more doing, but is *very* easy overall. So, don't let the science of planting seeds intimidate you.

Starting flowers from seed gives you greater access to different plant varieties. Not to mention, it's a rewarding experience to grow your own plants from seed—and a fun indoor gardening activity to do during the winter.

Depending on your climate and what plants you choose to grow, seeds can be started inside or outside. I'm going to show you how to do it both ways, but I recommend you start with easy ones outside first before investing in indoor seed-starting equipment. You should see if you like growing flowers from seed before you bite off more than you can chew.

While starting seeds indoors is easy to do, it's a little more involved than planting them outdoors. The good news is that you don't need a greenhouse because seed-starting can be done anywhere inside your home with minimal space and the right supplies.

MY FAVORITE FLOWERS TO GROW IN A CUT FLOWER GARDEN

Dahlia	Larkspur	Sweet pea	Cosmos	Strawflower
Zinnia	Calendula	Sunflower	Celosia	Snapdragon

How to Grow a Cut Flower Garden

Measure your garden space. Then calculate how many seed packets you need to buy based on the room you have and what you want to grow. Keep in mind that most flowers grown for cutting need at least six to eight hours of full sun.

You can also grow a cut flower garden in planters. Start the flowers from seed and when they are ready to plant, follow my container gardening tips in chapter 9.

Purchasing Seeds

For the best results, look for seeds from high-quality growers. You can purchase them online from reputable growers like Floret Flower Farm, Johnny's Selected Seeds, and Renee's Garden, or you can buy seeds at your local nursery.

Because it's easy to get caught up in the seed varieties available, think about how you want your garden to look and choose flowers based on bloom time, color, texture, and size before you shop. And be sure to save each seed packet, because you will refer to the directions on them often.

How to Calculate the Number of Seed Packets to Buy

To determine the number of seed packets to buy for a particular garden space, follow these steps:

- Measure the area of your garden to determine the total square footage (see chapter 2).

- Check the seed packet for the recommended planting distance between each seed. This will help you determine how many plants you can fit in your garden area.

- Seeds don't always germinate, so it's best to buy extra to make up for any losses. A good rule of thumb is to buy 10 to 20 percent beyond what you think you will need.

- Consider whether you want to have a large harvest or if you just want to grow a few plants for ornamental purposes.

I usually only buy one seed packet per variety. But if you want to grow flowers for cutting en masse or there are fewer seeds in the packet, you may want to get two packets. When in doubt, order up a packet instead of down. You can always store and save the extra seeds in a cool, dark place until the following growing season.

How to Start Seeds Indoors

If you are starting your seeds indoors, invest in good seed-starting equipment. Sure, you can try starting them near a sunny window without grow lights, but I've found much greater success when I use the right supplies.

Several years ago, I started seeds in a south-facing window, thinking that would provide them with enough light. And while I found some success, it wasn't much. Winter daylight hours are short. Plus, the front of my windows lacked space for the seedlings to get the right amount of light to grow well.

After a few years of ho-hum success, I invested in proper supplies to start seeds more easily in my basement under grow lights. And it was hugely successful! I started over 1,400 flowers that year. The investment had a big payoff, so I highly recommend setting yourself up with the right equipment if you want to start seeds indoors.

Supplies Needed

You can purchase premade growing systems, or you can make your own. Just make sure you can adjust the grow lights with ease. I hung grow lights on tiered wire shelves and bought almost everything I needed at a big-box store. So, do your research and buy or design a system that works best for you, your budget, and the space you have.

SEED STARTING SUPPLIES

Seeds	Pots or cell trays	Seed-starting potting soil	Programmable timer
Shelf system or table	Drainage trays		Watering can
Vermiculite	Oscillating fan	Heat mat	
Clear dome lids	Grow lights	Plant labels	

Seed-Starting Supply Tips

Purchase cell trays for each variety of seed you plan to start. I've made the mistake of condensing different plants and varieties in the same cell tray and because they germinated at different times, some never sprouted at all. So only start one variety per cell tray.

Reuse old pots and cell trays. Before reusing them, though, clean them really well with a 1:10 ratio of chlorine bleach to water to sanitize and kill off any pest or disease residue left behind.

Plan Your Schedule

Get yourself organized by writing seed start dates on a calendar and familiarizing yourself with their sowing requirements. Read each seed packet to determine when to sow each variety of seed by counting backward from the last frost date in your area. Then write down the type of flower, variety, date of maturity, when it should be sowed, seed-starting dates, size, and color.

Whether starting-seed indoors or out, the type of plant you're planning to grow plus your last frost date will help you determine when to start your seeds. Knowing this information will help you create a seed-start planning schedule that works for you and your garden.

How to Sow Seeds Indoors

Just before sowing seeds indoors, carefully read the information on each seed packet again because it may have specific sowing instructions for that particular plant. Some, like larkspur, have a chill requirement before sowing to aid in their germination. Others, like sweet peas, need to be presoaked for twenty-four hours before sowing. And others, like sunflowers or calendula, prefer direct sowing in the garden versus being sowed indoors.

In general, follow these instructions to sow seeds indoors. (And follow the directions on the seed packet if something different is specified.)

1. Premoisten the seed-starting soil in a separate tray or bucket.

2. Fill and pack down the soil in each cell or pot to remove air pockets.

3. Sow seeds according to the packet directions (typically planting them two times their depth).

4. Drop 1 to 2 seeds in each hole, then cover the holes with vermiculite. While you can also cover them with soil, vermiculite is easier to grow through.

5. Label each cell, tray, and pot well because you won't remember the varieties later.

6. Cover the pots or trays with a clear plastic dome or similar covering.

7. Many seeds germinate quicker on heat mats under grow lights. Use a timer and set grow lights to be on for 14 to 16 hours per day.

8. Watch for seed germination every day. Some varieties will take a few days, while others will take longer.

9. When seedlings emerge, remove the plastic covering and take them off the heat mats, even if they didn't all sprout, because more will germinate later.

10. Maintain seedlings under grow lights about an inch or so away from the tallest seedling. You'll need to adjust the lights as the seedlings grow.

11. Check the soil daily to make sure it stays evenly moist. Always water from the bottom so you don't damage seedlings by watering them from above. If you start seeds with a water reservoir, you can keep that filled. You can also set trays and pots in a pan filled with water for roughly an hour per day.

12. As seedlings grow, reread the seed packets to see if there are any special instructions, like pinching back the growing seedlings.

13. Use an oscillating fan set on low to promote air circulation.

14. Rotate trays or pots every so often to encourage seedlings to grow upright instead of leaning in one direction to reach the light.

Moving Seedlings Outdoors

About two weeks before the last frost date in your area, seedlings will need to be prepared for life outside. Because they were grown indoors, they need to be slowly transitioned to outdoor growing conditions. This process, called "hardening off," is a gradual exposure that will help prevent shock from temperature changes, wind, and sun exposure. So, don't skimp on this process.

While many seed starts need to be planted after the last frost date, some varieties can go in the ground a little earlier. Check each seed packet for cold hardiness so you know when to start this process.

How to Harden Off Seedlings

Hardening off seedlings is a little laborious, but it's pretty simple to do. Wait for a mild day that's at least 45 to 50 degrees before moving seedlings outside to a protected area in full shade. After two to three hours, move the seedlings back

SEED STARTING SCHEDULE

FLOWER/VEGETABLE TYPE & VARIETY

LAST FROST DATE

Days to Maturity

Sowing Information

Start Date

Height/Width

Color

Notes

inside a basement, heated garage, or shed.

Do this for about two to three days, then move the seedlings to a location where they will receive morning sun. Every few days, gradually increase their exposure to more sunlight. For seedlings to become strong, sturdy plants, this process is critical.

After two weeks of acclimation, your new plant babies should be able to live outside all the time. But watch the weather closely for unexpected frosts or freezes. They happen!

Hardening Off Quick Tips

- Too much sunlight too soon can cause leaf scorch.

- Avoid bringing seedlings outdoors on days with extreme weather like high winds or heavy rain. They aren't ready for it yet, so skip that day and resume the hardening-off process the next day.

- Protect seedlings if temperatures fall below 45 degrees by moving them indoors or placing them inside a cold frame. If you can't move them, be prepared to cover them with something like a crop cover.

How to Direct Sow Seeds Outdoors

If you are new to seed starting, I recommend getting your feet wet with easy-to-germinate seed varieties like sunflowers, nasturtiums, calendula, or zinnias to see how you like starting flowers from seed before going all-in.

When the last frost date arrives, direct sow seeds according to packet directions in prepared beds, cell trays, or peat pots with premoistened seed-starting soil. (If seeds require sowing before the last frost date, follow that timetable.) Unless you prepare the garden beds for seed starting, peat pots are great to use because you have more control over the soil and they can be directly planted in the ground without disturbing the seedlings. If your beds are mulched like mine, they are not ideal for sowing seeds, so peat pots are a great solution because you can just plant the whole thing in the ground after germination.

When working with peat pots, it's easier to group them in a tray to keep them corralled so they can be moved around and easily watered. Just be sure to label each pot so you know what seed is planted there. It is not necessary to use a plastic dome or other covering to aid with germination. Just let them do their thing as if you sowed seeds directly in the ground. Keep an eye on them so they don't dry out. If there is a heavy rain, you'll need to empty any water collecting in the bottom of the tray.

When planning out your garden, consider succession planting. This means sowing the same type of seeds every few days or a week apart to get an extended bloom time from flowers that are typically one and done, like sunflowers.

Depending on the year and what flowers I feel like growing, my usual outdoor direct-sow list includes sunflowers, calendula, tithonia, nasturtiums, cosmos, and zinnias.

Planting the Cut Flower Garden

Once your seedlings have been hardened off, it's time to plant them in the ground. If unexpected harsh, cold weather arrives after planting, you may want to protect young seedlings with a cold frame or crop cover. Unexpected heat can also damage plants.

When I grew my cut flower garden a few years ago, New Jersey experienced extreme heat for about a week shortly after I planted, so I watered my seedlings well so they wouldn't dry out. I've also seen gardeners provide shade tents to protect young plants. Extreme weather doesn't happen often, but you need to be ready for anything.

Provide Support for Tall and Heavy Flower Varieties

If plants are expected to grow more than two feet tall or have heavy flower heads, they may need additional support so they don't fall over. Some plants that need additional support are dahlias, zinnias, snapdragons, delphiniums, peonies, and cosmos. Of course, it depends on the variety, so make sure you read the seed packets or plant tags for recommendations.

In general, it's best to start supporting plants when they are about one foot tall. However, I recommend staking them *when you plant* because growth happens so quickly and, if you aren't paying attention, it can be tough to support them later. Since I've made this mistake myself, I recommend staking when you plant versus waiting until "the right time."

If you want less work, grow flowers that don't need that additional support.

Fertilizing

When seedlings are first planted in the ground, feed them with a fish emulsion fertilizer for the first week or two to give them a good start. After plants acclimate, which is usually around a week or so, I use a slow-release fertilizer.

How to Cut Fresh Flowers for Arrangements

Have you ever heard the saying, "The more you cut, the more they'll bloom?" That's pretty typical for flowers grown specifically for cutting.

To get the most out of your cut flowers, cut them early in the morning or later in the day when temperatures are cooler and the plants retain more water. Avoid cutting in the heat of the day because the cut blooms won't last as long in a bouquet. And always make sure your snips are clean in between cutting plants so you don't pass developing diseases from one plant to another. Here are some tips for cutting flowers from the garden:

- Bring a bucket of warm water with you to the garden.

- Select flowers that have buds which recently opened, if possible.

- Using clean, sharp pruners or snips, cut flowers at a 45-degree angle slightly above a side branch or where you see another flower branch forming. Cut the foliage off of the stems as you work so the leaves don't sit in the water and rot.

- Immediately put the cut flowers in water. It's best to let them stay in the bucket of water for a few hours in a cool, shaded location to prepare them for life in an arrangement before you style them.

How to Arrange Flowers

Choose a container like a vase or a bowl and fill it halfway with warm water. Use a floral frog, floral tape, or even Scotch Tape to help keep the flowers sturdy in the arrangement. If you are using tape, create a grid pattern.

Remove all the leaves and lower stems of the flower that will sit in any water. Anything left under the waterline will rot and cause the flowers to decline. Make a fresh cut on a 45-degree angle just before dropping the stem in the arrangement. This will keep the stems from sitting flat and promote better water consumption.

The general rule of thumb is to cut flowers roughly one and a half to two times the height of the container you want to use. Use the thriller, filler, and spiller method of design for aesthetically pleasing arrangements. But you can also create a bouquet that looks aesthetically pleasing to you.

Quick Tips to Keep Flowers Fresh Longer

- Always start with a clean vase or floral foam.
- Prepare each flower for the arrangement.
- Feed the flowers with flower food (see below) once they have been arranged.
- Keep the water clean by changing it every 2 to 3 days.
- Recut the stems when you change the water.
- Keep freshly cut flowers in a cool, dry place away from the heat and out of direct sunlight.

How to Make Fresh Cut Flower Food

While you can purchase cut flower food, you can easily make it yourself with this quick recipe. In one quart of lukewarm water, mix in two crushed aspirin, one teaspoon of sugar, and a few drops of bleach to kill harmful bacteria. Stir until everything is dissolved, and add one cup of this flower food to top off your vase once all the flowers are arranged.

As with beginning any kind of new garden, my best advice is to start small when undertaking seed starting for the first time. Keep it simple, get your feet wet, and build confidence. The larger the cut flower garden is, the more work it will be.

Plant flowers that are easy to grow, spark joy, and that you'll love seeing inside your home. You will leave this experience with an incredible sense of satisfaction that you grew something beautiful from seed to flower. And you'll enjoy the experience that much more if you are realistic about the amount of work you want to do. A fun and manageable experience the first time will help you feel eager to try more next year.

BEST EASY-CARE CUT FLOWERS TO GROW

If you are just beginning to grow a cut flower garden, try starting these plants from seed because they are easy to start, grow, and maintain, and they can all be direct sown outdoors and generally do not require staking (depending on the variety).

| Nasturtium | Zinnia | Sunflower | Celosia | Calendula |

CHAPTER ELEVEN

A Successful Easy-Care Garden

—

If you are a new gardener or think you kill things, it seems like there's so much to learn. Am I right? But once you understand the basics and just start doing the things, you'll become a more confident and successful gardener.

And eventually, gardening will become second nature to you.

There will be lots of trial and error along the way. Don't get down on yourself when things don't go right. Some plants will thrive, and others won't. It's all a part of the gardening experience, and you've got to remind yourself that it is okay if a plant fails.

You are not a bad gardener. You are not a plant killer. And you can still grow flowers with success. Say that again on repeat, because it is true.

There are some things we have control over when growing a garden—some basics that, when followed, will take the home gardener down a path of success.

And believe me when I tell you, I haven't always followed the basics, and I've made almost every one of the following mistakes at some point in my gardening career. Don't beat yourself up if you've made any or even all of these mistakes.

Even the best gardeners—myself included!—still make mistakes, whether it's cutting corners, neglecting to properly care for plants, or not learning enough about new plants before diving in.

Here are some helpful tips to keep in mind so you can get the most out of your garden.

Remember the Basics

Whenever you plant a garden, whether it is in the ground, a raised bed, or a container, keep the gardening basics in mind. It's easy to rush through them because we just want to buy flowers and plant them, but you'll save yourself some heartache later if you think about things first.

Know what zone you are in, test your soil, and try to plant things that are native to your area, because they are easier to grow. Check the amount of sun, water, and space your plants need, so it's less work for you in the long run.

Fifteen Mistakes to Avoid

The following common gardening mistakes are listed in no particular order.

1. Not knowing your correct hardiness zone
2. Not testing your soil
3. Not keeping recommended plant spacing in mind
4. Overwatering
5. Underwatering
6. Planting in the wrong location
7. Planting non-native plants
8. Not reading and saving plant tags
9. Taking on more than you can handle
10. Not weeding
11. Not inspecting plants before buying them at the nursery
12. Not considering the critters
13. Not caring for plants while you're on vacation
14. Not planting near a water source
15. Not giving your plants good nutrition

As you gain experience, these things will become second nature. Keep the basics in mind and you will be well on your way to growing a successful, easy-care garden.

Be Realistic About Your Lifestyle

Have you ever heard the saying, "Don't bite off more than you can chew"?

This advice applies to gardening. There is some work involved with planting, growing, and maintaining a garden, so start small, learn, and expand your gardens as you gain experience.

Practice, learn, and adapt as you go.

I know how tempting it is to "go big or go home" in the spring when we are all itching to get outside and take on new projects. We don't mind doing all the things in the spring because there's a sense of immediate gratification to see new plants in the ground, and the weather is mild. But in the summer, you'll often be watering and weeding in really hot weather. When the chill of winter and the dormant season approaches, you want to look back on your garden and think, *That was amazing!*—not collapse in exhaustion, saying, *I am never doing that again.*

Keep the Plant Tags

While they are easy to toss, those little plant tags carry vital information that includes light requirements, size, bloom times, and variety. You can save them in a garden journal or notebook file. Or, even easier, take a photo of them and save them in an album on your phone for easy reference.

I can't tell you how many times I've gone back to a plant not knowing what the variety is. Saving that plant tag in a garden journal or on your phone will make a big difference in the future. Trust me—you will not always remember the variety you planted.

Pull Every Weed

This is a big one. Yes, you have to weed, and it's best to do it as you go instead of waiting until it's a major, all-weekend chore.

There's no easy way around it—weeding has to be done. Hand pulling or hoeing is the best method for weeding gardens. Please don't use toxic chemicals to remove weeds. They are really bad for the environment, bad for your garden, bad for the water table, bad for your pets and other wildlife, and most importantly, bad for you and your family's health. Toxic chemicals are just *bad*.

If you don't pull weeds, your garden will become overgrown. Weeds zap nutrients from your plants and flowers. And even worse, some weeds can totally take over your garden in a big, bad way that will force you to rip out all your plants and start again from scratch. This happened to me once, and it was a total disaster.

Several years ago, well after I became a master gardener and should have known better, I was busy running around with my kids when I saw a yellow threading weed growing around my perennial plants in the front yard cottage garden. I kept putting off dealing with it because I didn't have the time or energy to pull it out. In fact, I wasn't even sure what it was, and I didn't bother to check.

Well, I waited so long that this weed threaded its way through my garden, winding around all my perennial plants. When I finally researched what it was (a parasitic vine called dodder) and how to get rid of it, it was so bad and extended throughout so much of my garden that I had to rip out all the affected plants along with the dodder. As a result, there was a huge gaping

PRO TIP: If you are vacationing in the summer, pull container gardens into the shade while you are away so they don't dry out as quickly. Just remember to put them back in their original locations when you return home, so they get their preferred amount of sun.

hole in my garden for a very long time. And it took a few years to eradicate the dodder as well.

I was really upset with myself.

Don't make my mistake. Put on some good tunes, get out in your garden, and stay on top of those weeds! It will totally be worth your time. And remember, the smaller the garden, the easier it will be to keep up with the weeding.

Inspect Plants Before Bringing Them Home from the Nursery

Before bringing a plant home from the nursery, always check it out. Make sure you don't see any bugs on the leaves, stems, or in the soil, and check the undersides of the foliage for signs of disease, such as yellowing or fungal spots. The last thing you want to do is bring a plant home that has pest and disease problems and spread it to the rest of your garden.

If you can, remove the plant from the nursery pot while you're still in the store and check the root system to see how rootbound it is and how healthy the roots are. If the roots look soft, mushy, and decayed, don't buy it.

I have put many plants back on the shelf after inspecting them. Don't be afraid to check the plants, and leave bad plants at the nursery, even if it is something you really want in your garden. It's not worth it, and you can likely find a healthier version of that same plant elsewhere.

Assess Your Landscape for Critters

Deer are a huge problem in my area, so I have to take certain steps to deer-proof my garden and choose plants they prefer not to eat. But I've also had problems with rodents, rabbits, chipmunks, groundhogs, squirrels, and birds.

Keep a close eye on your garden. Walk the beds every day to catch wildlife problems early. We can't always prevent damage, but we can learn to garden around them.

And just because deer decimated something you planted five years ago doesn't mean you can't ever grow a pretty flower garden that they'll leave alone. It just means you have to be smarter about it by planting things they don't like or protecting your plants a little more.

Some local friends of mine had this very problem, and I was able to plant containers and garden beds for them that were never touched by their resident deer. So, it is very possible to create a critter-proof garden.

Care for Your Garden While You're on Vacation

Before going away, even if it's just for a weekend, make sure your garden has the care it needs to survive while you are gone, particularly during the hot summer months.

The last thing you want to do is spend months working on a garden, only to let it dry out over a few days while you're getting some rest and relaxation. Set timers on a watering system, ask a friend to help out while you are away, or find a neighbor who wants to earn a little extra money for their own summer fun.

Plant Near a Water Source

Before starting a garden, know where your water source is located so you can site your garden as close to it as possible. That way, it will be much easier for you to keep up with watering plants.

If a water source is really far away, it will be tough to establish new plants or keep them hydrated during the summer heat. Even with the best of intentions and attention, your garden will be more difficult to care for in the blazing summer heat than it was when you began in early spring.

My former vegetable garden was really far away from a water source, and it was hard to keep that garden watered in July and August. As a result, my vegetable harvest suffered from inconsistent watering. Don't make the same mistake I did. Really think about where that water source is located and how you will get water to your plants.

It is no fun to drag a 50- to 100-foot hose around throughout the growing season. If you have to, you have to, but I don't recommend it.

Keep Plants Nourished with Healthy Soil and Plant Food

Starting and maintaining healthy soil is vital for growing a happy garden that blooms. Adding compost and other soil amendments yearly will organically feed and nurture your garden. And topping those beds off with wood mulch not only suppresses weeds, but also breaks down and amends the soil too.

If you are feeding annuals and container gardens with a slow-release fertilizer, make sure you note when the next feeding will be so you don't forget the follow-up application. Those plants need it to continue producing an abundance of flowers.

And if you are using a weekly liquid feed, make sure you keep up on your plant feeding schedule.

Keep Planting, Keep Growing, Keep Learning

Now that we've reached the end of our journey together, I want to leave you with this thought.

It is okay to fail.

I say this on repeat because, like I said in the beginning of this book, plants come and go and gardening is a learning experience.

After more than twenty-five years, I'm still learning.

We will make mistakes. Some plants will thrive and do well. Others will die. We will sometimes get lazy with our gardening practices. Don't take it to heart. It doesn't make you a bad gardener when things go wrong. In fact, just the opposite is true. You are becoming a better gardener.

I realize some of the basics sound daunting to learn, but once you've mastered them? It really is pretty easy.

With each plant we grow, we learn. We learn how easy or fussy that plant is, how it performs in our garden, and whether or not that plant is even worth our time. I've planted lots of flowers that I've never planted again because they didn't perform as well as others. So, don't focus on what doesn't work. Focus on the plants that do well in your garden, the plants that require just enough care, and the plants that complement your lifestyle.

When my kids were younger, there were some flowers that required more from me as a gardener than I could give, and I let those plants fail or didn't grow them at all. I've also planted supposedly easy-care perennials that never returned the following season.

It happens.

Not everything goes our way. So don't beat yourself up over it—just try a different plant next time! There are so many out there that will be better suited for you and your garden.

I could tell you all the plants I love, and you could try them and have a completely different experience. And that's okay! That's part of the fun—learning what works best for you, your lifestyle, and your garden.

Stay Positive

It's really easy to get in a negative mindset if something doesn't work out. Because let's face it, it's much easier to say, "I can't do it . . . I'm not good at it . . . plants don't like me" than to pause, reflect, troubleshoot, and do it differently.

Growing flowers is a very forgiving and enjoyable hobby to undertake. Once you get started, you'll wonder why it took you so long to begin. There's a flower for everyone to grow. The challenge is finding the right plants that work with your lifestyle and your garden. If you don't know where to begin, start with one easy-care plant that will grow with the conditions you have.

I hope this book gave you a starting point to begin and just do. Often, the first step to changing something in your life is to change your mindset. Keep planting, keep growing, keep learning, and you can grow the flower garden of your dreams.

GLOSSARY OF TERMS

acidic soil—soil pH is less than 7

aerating soil—loosening up the soil to promote air circulation and easier planting

alkaline soil—soil pH is greater than 7

annual—plants that complete their whole life cycle from seed to flower within one year

backfilling—filling in the area around plant roots with soil when planting

bed—a defined garden area that is separate from the uncultivated landscape

beneficial insect or wildlife—insect or animal that eats or destroys harmful garden insects or pests

border—a defined garden area, separate from the landscape, that contains more than one plant type

compost—organic materials from yard and kitchen waste that have been mixed and decomposed into a rich, soil-like substance

cottage garden—an informal garden design that has a natural, relaxed look with plants growing in a seemingly haphazard manner

cutting back—removing or cutting off foliage, flower buds, or deadheads to rejuvenate a plant, control its size, improve the aesthetic, or promote new growth and flowering

cutting garden—a garden that is specifically grown to harvest cut flowers

deadheading—the process of removing spent or dead flowers from a plant

dividing plants—separating a larger plant into smaller sections so each has its own root system, thus creating new plants

evergreen—a plant that retains its foliage color throughout the year

edging—cleaning up a garden's edge between the yard and the garden space so grass roots do not grow into the garden bed

edging plants—a row of small, mounding plants that softens the lines around the edge of a bed or border

existing soil—the soil in a garden that is already there before any amendments or new soil have been added

fertilizer—organic or nonorganic material applied to the soil that provides essential nutrients, such as nitrogen, phosphorus, and potassium, in order to help plants grow and develop properly

formal garden—a garden design with straight, clean lines where the plants are arranged with symmetry

frost date—approximate date of the first or last plant-killing frost in spring and fall

growing habit—the way a plant grows and develops in shape, size, and form

groundcover—typically, a low-growing plant that grows laterally and covers the soil surface

hardening off—the process of acclimating plants from indoor to outdoor growing conditions

invasive plant—a plant that grows, spreads, and reproduces so much that it overtakes a garden or surrounding habitat and becomes a nuisance

leaf mold compost—a material made from fallen leaves that forms a rich, crumbly, soil-like substance high in organic matter and low in nutrients; used as a soil amendment in gardens and landscapes to improve soil structure and water-holding capacity while acting as a mulch

loam—medium-texture soil that contains a moderate amount of clay, sand, and silt

local cooperative extension—a branch of the Cooperative Extension System, which is a nationwide educational network that provides practical, research-based knowledge and assistance to people and communities; home gardeners can call the local master gardener hotline for help with plant identification and other garden issues

microclimate—a small, defined area with temperatures, humidity levels, and wind patterns that differ from the surrounding environment, which can influence what can be grown in that particular location; for example, a valley may have a different microclimate than a nearby hilltop

mulch—material applied to the soil surface that helps retain moisture, suppress weeds, and maintain an even soil temperature

native plant—a plant that naturally grows in a specific area or climate and has likely been around for hundreds or even thousands of years

neutral soil—soil pH of exactly 7

nitrogen—nutrient that promotes growth with a focus on lush, green foliage instead of flowers

node—the location on a plant stem from which buds, leaves, and branches originate

organic matter—material derived from living matter, such as compost and mulches that have decomposed

perennial—plants that live more than two years, typically are cold-hardy, die back late in the year, and return the following growing season

pH—a measure of the acidity or alkalinity of soil that is expressed on a scale of 0 to 14, with 7 being neutral

pinching—using snips or your finger and thumb to remove growing tips, stems, or the first set of leaves from a plant, thereby promoting branchier, fuller growth

plant hardiness—a plant's ability to grow in adverse environmental conditions, such as cold temperatures, drought, heavy rainfall, or high winds

prolonged blooming—extended flowering time of a plant

propagation—the process of creating new plants from existing ones, either through seed-sowing, taking cuttings, dividing, or other methods

rebloom—a second set of flowers on a plant; usually smaller, shorter in duration, and less prolific than the first set

reseeding or self-seeding—the process of a plant dropping seeds that will germinate and grow into new plants without any human intervention

rootbound—a condition where plant roots have become tightly packed and restricted due to a plant outgrowing its contained space; typically with roots growing in a circle inside the root ball instead of outward into the soil

seed heads—dried clusters of ripe seeds that appear on a plant after flowering; some look beautiful when left to remain on the plant in the winter; wildlife often eat them

shaping—pruning a plant in a rounded or other formal shape

shearing—cutting back or pruning a plant with hedge shears or clippers

soil structure—the way in which clay, silt, and sand assemble together in the soil

soil texture—the proportions of clay, silt, and sand in the soil

soil amendments—materials added to the soil to improve its physical and chemical properties; amendments can be organic or inorganic and are used to enhance soil fertility, improve soil structure, increase water-holding capacity, or adjust soil pH

staking— the process of supporting plant stems to keep them upright and prevent them from bending or falling over

stalk—plant stems that hold the plant's leaves, flowers, and fruit (if any)

suckers—growths that appear from the root systems of shrubs or trees that may compete with the main stem for resources such as water and nutrients, leading to reduced growth or fruiting

transplanting—moving a plant or plant division from one location to another

USDA Hardiness Zone—a system used by the United States Department of Agriculture (USDA) to classify the average minimum winter temperatures for different regions across the country; the information is helpful for selecting plants that are likely to survive the winter and thrive in a specific climate

variety—a subdivision of a species with the same inheritable characteristics

water sprouts—shoots that arise from the trunk or upper branches of a tree or shrub, often upright, more susceptible to diseases or pests, and not as fruitful as the natural growth

Extension services

Many universities have extension sites. Find one near you for good local information, but I have found helpful information from sites across the country. Here are some I have used:

njaes.rutgers.edu/pubs/

extension.psu.edu/

gardening.cornell.edu/homegardening/

gardeningsolutions.ifas.ufl.edu/plants/

extension.missouri.edu/

extension.psu.edu/trees-lawns-and-landscaping/home-gardening

extension.msstate.edu/lawn-and-garden

extension.oregonstate.edu/gardening

extension.umn.edu/yard-and-garden

communityenvironment.unl.edu/

extension.usu.edu/yardandgarden/

hgic.clemson.edu/

hort.extension.wisc.edu

hortnews.extension.iastate.edu/

mbgna.umich.edu/

plants.ces.ncsu.edu/

utgardens.tennessee.edu/

canr.msu.edu/home_gardening/flowers/

Another very helpful website is provenwinners.com. The site has a wealth of information, and I have had great success with their plants.

ACKNOWLEDGMENTS

Starting my blog and writing this book have been an incredible journey that I could not have done without the love, support, and encouragement from so many amazing people in my life.

To my husband, Chris, none of this would be possible without your tremendous support, hard work, and faith. Thank you for going along with all my big ideas and helping me execute them. From supporting my gardening habit, to spending full weekends starting new beds, to uprooting our family to a new home because "it felt right to me," thank you for just going with it and being the best friend that you are.

For my daughters, Mackenzie, Shana, and Tori, I feel incredibly blessed to have raised such smart, fun, and caring young women. I'm so proud to be your mom and I can't thank you enough for helping me at home while I wrote this book. Dream, think big, keep a positive mindset always, and you will go far and be successful in life no matter what you do.

Thanks to my fur-besties for hanging out with me all day every day and for not crushing my flowers every time you run through the beds.

Thank you to my niece Sutton, who assists with the blog and helped do research for this book.

To my mom, Marilyn, and to Elisa, Nora, Laura, and the rest of our family, thank you for believing in me, encouraging me every step of the way, and supporting my journey from wife and mom to blogger and author.

Thank you to my mother-in-law, Pat, who helped stock our first home with her garden flowers. Your excitement to tour the gardens each time you visit means the world to me.

Thank you, Clay, we could not have made the move to the new house without you.

Arden, Margaret, Nancy, Bonnie, Karen, my book club, and all the other friends who I've been tight with through the years, your friendship means the world to me. This book was written specifically for you—with every word written, I thought of you all.

Thank you, Caroline, for inspiring me just to grow things.

To my amazing blog coach, KariAnne, your guidance and support helped me grow my blog and brand, which made it possible to write this book.

Thank you to Jennifer, Rachel, Anne, AnnMarie, Kim, and the rest of my blogging friends, for your support, encouragement, and friendship. I am fortunate to be part of your tribe.

Huge thanks to my amazing gardener, Victor, who helps bring my ideas to life and keeps my expansive gardens under control.

Thanks to Mark for helping Chris build all the things over many weekends to make our home and gardens amazing.

To Ruth, Heather, Heidi, and the Harvest House Publishers team, thank you for your friendship, encouragement, insight, and guidance. But most of all, thank you for believing in me and helping me bring this book to life.

Thank you to my faithful Bricks 'n Blooms readers on both the blog and socials for your daily support, encouragement, and comments. I could not have asked for a better community to share my love for gardening with, and I thank you from the bottom of my heart.

And finally, a huge thank you to all of you who are reading this book. I am thrilled you are here, and I hope you find a love for growing flowers too.

Stacy Ling is a blogger and master gardener who has been growing flowers and plants for more than 25 years. She found her joy in gardening while pursuing a law degree. After passing the bar exam and working in tax for a few years, Stacy and her husband, Christopher, moved to the New Jersey suburbs, where she developed a deep passion for all things plants and flowers.

Stacy became a master gardener through the Rutgers Cooperative Extension and started her own garden design business as she helped friends and neighbors plant and grow their own gardens.

Stacy started her garden and home blog in 2018 and has grown her brand, *Bricks 'n Blooms*, by regularly sharing gardening, DIY, and home decor content, as well as easy recipes and entertaining ideas. You can also find her on Bloom TV Network, where she shares tips, tricks, and inspiration.

Stacy's gardens have been featured by *Horticulture* magazine, *Fine Gardening* magazine, *Wine Enthusiast* magazine, and she was a finalist in the 2022 *Cottages and Bungalows* Curb Appeal Contest. She has appeared on *The Life and Style Podcast* and *Living Large in a Small House* podcast.

In fall 2021, Stacy and her husband purchased the home of their dreams in nearby central New Jersey. They moved with their three daughters to an 1850 farmhouse situated on ten acres with expansive gardens, tree sculptures, and statues.